Dedicated to Judy and Roberta

Who is rich? a Talmudic sage was asked.
He who has a wise and beautiful wife.

CRY A LITTLE, LAUGH A LOT

14 Original One-Act Plays
by Milton Polsky and Allan Yashin

Published by Blue Thread,
an imprint of JEWISH CURRENTS magazine

Blue Thread Communications

Cover design by Lawrence Bush

ISBN 978-0-9903524-1-9

Allan and Milton encourage royalty-free productions of these plays.
If you plan to produce any of the plays, please make inquiries to:
Millan Manage-Mint
Polskyspen@aol.com
AY100641@aol.com

Acknowledgments

First and foremost, our gratitude to the ladies who were with us every step of this journey. For their steadfast support and editorial acuity, Allan thanks his wife, Judy; and Milton, likewise, thanks his wife, Roberta, and daughter, Maddy Neely, for their staunch support. Before they read our words in this book, they heard them spoken in our homes or in some very special places where the plays were presented. Hence, our enduring appreciation of the following talented actors associated with the UFT (United Federation of Teachers) Players: Annette Adler, Ilene Bauer, Pat Brophy, Charles Castrovinci, James Cunningham, Suzanne Engel, Barbara Haspel, Ronald Hainey, Basil Joseph, Jack Koppel, Suzanne Lamberg, Keren Liswood, Cathy Parsons, Elizabeth Rosen, Gail Sherwood, Ken Solway, Hanna Stark, Warren Wyss, Daniel Wasserman, and Lolly Yacker Winderbaum.

Other actors who have performed in our plays include the East Side Players' Andrew Benjamin, Tory Meringoff, Roberta Feldhusen, Roy Feldhusen, and Jen Silverman. Thanks for the support of Carlos Jerome of Around the Block and their actors who performed so well in our shows: Elizabeth Bove, Pat Franklin, Joe Albert Lima, and Barry Sacker. Many thanks to our fine directors: Suzanne Lamberg, Andreas Robertz, Elizabeth Rosen, and Lolly Yacker Winderbaum. Kudos to all who participated in the productions as crews and producers.

Bravo to the photographers, Andrew Benjamin, George Miller Associates, and Roberta Polsky. Our deep appreciation to Paul Sugarman, publisher of Puck Press, for his permission to reprint in this volume "Shakes Hands," originally published in *A Shakespeare Trilogy: Three Apocryphal Tales of How the Bard Wrote His Plays.* A bouquet of heartfelt thanks to Howard Berland, whose helping pen enhanced a number of Milt's plays. Special thanks to the wonderfully attentive librarian and custodial staff of the Epiphany Library in New York whose hospitality to the East Side Players was peerless. UFT staff members, including supervisor George Altomare, Nyree McCrea, Charles Dudley, Derrick and Ricky, were always so helpful. We would like to also thank the stellar staff of the UFT Si Beagle Retirement Lifelong Learning program, where a number of our plays were first read in workshops, providing us with valuable feedback. Thanks to the UFT *New York Teacher* for permission to use several photographs.

Finally, we are indebted to the audiences who saw our plays and by so doing helped to make them breathe and pulsate with life. They also gave us useful feedback. Lawrence Bush of Blue Thread put it all together with his usual elegant expertise. Our deep appreciation to them all.

Contents

Introduction 1

The Plays

Rhineland Bastard 5

An interracial couple, applying to adopt a child in Milwaukee in 1961, experiences discrimination. When the black husband reveals his fate under Hitler, their chances for adoption change radically.

First We Have the Bris, Then We Eat the Brisket 13

To Aaron and Marsha's surprise, planning an age-old ritual to celebrate a blessed event can lead to unexpected complications.

Shakes Hands 17

A Jewish merchant, returning to England during the Expulsion, seeks Shakespeare's help to find his runaway daughter. Might the Bard's compassion for the old man inspire one of his future plays?

A Chance Encounter 31

In the 1936 Olympics swimming trials at the Astoria, Queens pool, the biggest competition is not in the water.

I Feel Their Pain 39

Protests on Wall Street rekindle amorous passions aroused when Morris and Cynthia first met during a protest rally in Central Park in the '60s.

A Stroll in the Garden 49

At the Hebrew Home for the Aged, two sisters confront each other about whether their mother should sing a Yiddish song for Sir Rudolf Bing, who is also a resident in the Alzheimer Care Wing.

Mister Mitzvah Maker 57

It takes a little heavenly assistance to repair the heartbreak Samuel has caused at home.

The Empty Seder Chair 71

Right after the Civil War ends, a Jewish family invites Lincoln to their seder. While waiting for the president to arrive, their son reveals the anguish he experienced as a combat officer.

Chekhov, Shmekhov 85

Professor Philip Gruber, director of innovative productions of the works of Anton Chekhov, finds surprising inspiration from a new collaboration with the Russian songbird, Vera Similitude.

The Polish Girl 97

Has Martin finally found his niece after a twenty-year search?

The Kiddush Cup 109

Will this be Rabbi Singleton's final blessing as he faces a life-changing crisis in his shul?

The Late Bloomers 119

Paul and Amy get the surprise of their lives when they visit his elderly parents.

Exit the Maven from Mott Haven 127

Uncle Morris clashes with his nephew about going to a nursing home after living forty years in his South Bronx apartment. Morris recalls the games at Yankee Stadium and the pain he felt about his son serving in Vietnam.

The Pre-Bre Agreement 139

After thirty years of marriage, Sam and Sara would never think of getting a divorce. But a Pre-Bre Agreement couldn't hurt . . . could it?

Production History of the Plays 147

More Plays by the Authors 149

About the Authors 151

Introduction

(ALLAN and MILTON are sitting at Au Bon Pain, drinking coffee and brainstorming ideas for their Introduction to the book.)

ALLAN

Let's see, maybe start with something about how short our plays are.

MILTON

Sounds good . . .

ALLAN

Short *is* good. Who said it anyway, "Sorry my letter's so long, but I didn't have the time to write a short one?"

MILTON

I don't know, Allan, so many get the credit — Mark Twain, Shaw . . . I think Pascal was the first one to say it . . .

ALLAN

Yeah, the French philosopher — Quite a story there —

MILTON

So, what happened — ?

ALLAN

. . . Louis XIV, right, asked Pascal what a miracle is . . . And Pascal, without a moment's hesitation, shoots back, "The Jews — Absolutely, the Jews — "

MILTON

He said, "Absolutely"?

ALLAN

You're asking me, Milt? I wasn't around —

MILTON

Hey, not such a miracle that we could still laugh at ourselves, considering all the obstacles —

ALLAN

Well, drama and comedy sometimes together —

MILTON

Like life and theatre, they go together—

ALLAN

A little like us putting this collection together. I hope readers enjoy our efforts. Do you think some folks might even wish to stage the plays, with our blessings, of course?

MILTON

Well, they don't have to be Jewish to do so — to at least read 'em.

ALLAN

(Toasting with cups)

Not at all . . . but it couldn't hurt . . . L'Chaim!

MILTON

You know, Allan, we seem to agree on everything. That hardly seems Jewish at all.

ALLAN

Right, Milt, except I've been meaning to tell you I think my plays should come first in the book.

MILTON

Are you a little mishuga? My plays carry important messages. Yours are just filled with humor —

ALLAN

Be reasonable, everybody likes a good laugh.

MILTON

We'll see how funny you think it is when you hear from my attorney!

(They start to stand up in mock anger, facing each other, then smile as the lights fade.)

The Plays

Rhineland Bastard

Milton Polsky

Photo by George Miller Associates

André's passionate goal is challenged.

CHARACTERS

André Talgina, black, speaks with slight French accent, 35

Hedda Talgina, white, speaks with slight Polish accent, 35

Mrs. Vivian Reynolds, social worker, white, 60-65

PLACE AND TIME

The South Side Orphanage, Milwaukee, Wisconsin. A sparse room with a small table and three chairs. Late spring, 1961

(HEDDA is seated at the table, leafing through a photo album.)

HEDDA

(Flipping pages)
Lovely children. It's hard to choose.

MRS. REYNOLDS

Take your time, dear.

HEDDA

Oh, this little boy — so adorable . . .

(She shows MRS. REYNOLDS the page.)

MRS. REYNOLDS

His name is Andrew. He's three years old.

HEDDA

Andrew. Andy. It's so close to André! . . . That's my husband, he'll be here in a moment.

MRS. REYNOLDS

Yes, of course, you must choose together. Then we can start the procedure. You could probably have Andrew in time to celebrate the Fourth of July together.

(ANDRÉ enters. MRS. REYNOLDS, suppressing surprise upon seeing him, stands to greet him.)

ANDRÉ

Excuse me, I finally found a spot on Pulaski Drive. Sorry I'm late.

(He shakes hands with MRS. REYNOLDS. They both sit.)

MRS. REYNOLDS

(Nodding, picking up the folder)
Mr. Talgina, your application form says you were in a concentration camp in Germany. I thought, well, naturally, that you were . . .

ANDRÉ

White? Actually, Mrs. Reynolds, thousands of black people lived in Germany before the war.

MRS. REYNOLDS

Oh?

HEDDA

My husband I met right after the war. 1945. Just fifteen years ago. I am Polish. A nurse. After the war, he was in the DP — displaced persons . . . I helped nurse him back, in the camp. *(Smiling at the memory)* We were both so young.
(Silence)

MRS. REYNOLDS

I understand . . . if you'll excuse me for a moment.

(She briskly picks up the photo album and goes to the back room, offstage.)

HEDDA

Oh . . .

ANDRÉ

She's prejudiced. I can see it in her eyes, the way she looked at us. She had no idea who I was.

HEDDA

Shh, let me do the talking, darling, please.

(MRS. REYNOLDS returns, holding a different album.)

MRS. REYNOLDS

May I ask, Mr. Talgina, how did you find yourself in a concentration camp?

HEDDA

He didn't find himself there. The Nazis sent him there. Do you mind if I tell — from the beginning?

MRS. REYNOLDS

Yes, but . . . you are a Negro, sir. Correct? Do you call yourself that?

HEDDA

André's dad's family originally came from what is now Tanzania — off the southern coast of Africa. It was a German colony, then, and his father served with German troops in Europe.

MRS. REYNOLDS

Really? Go on, please.

HEDDA

Well . . . At the end of the First World War, the French occupied the German Rhineland, and many Africans — among the French, and a few among the Germans, both — hundreds of them ended up married to German women.

ANDRÉ

Including my father.

MS. REYNOLDS

(Picking up her pen)

So your parents were an interracial couple, correct?

ANDRÉ

As my wife and I are now! Yes! May I ask, Mrs. Reynolds, how this has anything to do . . . how might it — how do you say it — impede us from adopting a child?

MRS. REYNOLDS

I did not say that, sir. But we do have to be careful, for the benefit of all, but especially for the child.

HEDDA

André, there's a lovely little boy in their other book of photos. His name is Andrew.

ANDRÉ

So where did he go? Mrs. Reynolds, why did you take the book with Andrew?

HEDDA

(Softly, admonishing)

André . . .

ANDRÉ

Please listen to me, Mrs. Reynolds: I have a good job with a florist company here in Milwaukee — you can check.

MRS. REYNOLDS

Yes, for Fergusen Flowers — I saw that on your application. We use them.

ANDRÉ

I help with the arrangements, sometimes. I make deliveries. I work hard, long hours — union man, Teamsters.

(Trying to lighten it up)

No parking tickets, not one . . . My wife works, too, as a nurse. We can provide well for the child—

MRS. REYNOLDS

And do you plan to live where you are now, on the North Side?

HEDDA

Yes, for now. Later, perhaps later when we have more money saved we can buy a house.

MRS. REYNOLDS

On the South Side, or still on the North Side?

ANDRÉ

Where the colored live? Is that what you're saying? I assure you, there are many white children, too, on the North Side. But when I go into people's houses to make my deliveries, it doesn't make a difference which house it is. There's the same happiness, or the same mourning going on, the same hope, the same love! What does it matter, where we live? I assure you, it didn't make a difference in that camp I was in, where the Jews and all the others were dying next to each other!

HEDDA

André, please—

ANDRÉ

No, she must know things about me — they're not in your folder there, Mrs. Reynolds. I hope you don't think we are only capable of raising a black child, do you—?

MRS. REYNOLDS

No, I . . .

ANDRÉ

Or is it that you have trouble finding parents for black children here? So we don't get a choice, hm? Is this not America? 1961? Do we not have this new, young president, who says we have a right to choose, to act freely?

MRS. REYNOLDS

Mr. Talgina, you're in a private orphanage. We have the right to select our own clients! Now, do you or do you not wish to look through this album?

HEDDA

(Looking through the album)

Please, André, look with me . . . these are beautiful children, too.

ANDRÉ

Of course they are — but why are they separate, in their own albums? I want to see the other album, Mrs. Reynolds — the one with Andrew.

MRS. REYNOLDS

I told you, what's best for the child. There are certain policies we have in place. I am an employee here, and I . . .

ANDRÉ

And I am a fighter, Mrs. Reynolds. Listen to me. I was seven years old, not much older than many of the children in this album, when Hitler came to power. I was fourteen when his War of Hell broke out. I escaped to France and fought with the French Underground, because the policies of the Nazis had taken my future from me . . .

(He chokes up, breathes slowly, recovers composure.)

I have no idea even what happened to my parents. Some blacks were forced to join Hitler's army, so who knows, we may have been shooting at each another! Then the S.S. caught me and sent me to their bloody Dachau, in Germany.

(He rolls up his sleeve. MRS. REYNOLDS looks and recoils. He rolls back the sleeve. Silence.)

MRS. REYNOLDS

(Starts to rise)

I wish I could help you . . . Please, take your time with the album.

HEDDA

And Andrew?

MRS. REYNOLDS

Andrew is spoken for, I'm afraid. But I'm sure you'll find another.

(She collects her papers.)

ANDRÉ

Does nothing I've said mean anything to you?

MRS. REYNOLDS

Mr. Talgina, we have other clients waiting for me.

(She hesitates at door.)

Sometimes, in life, with certain circumstances in mind, there are no choices . . . no arrangements to be made because certain policies are the way they are . . . and we deal with it.

(She starts to exit.)

ANDRÉ

Mrs. Reynolds —

MRS. REYNOLDS

I'm very sorry, Mr. Talgina.

ANDRÉ

You are right. What you just said. Sometimes we cannot choose — as when Hitler forced every mixed-race child in the Rhineland to be sterilized for his dream of stamping out race pollution. I was one of those children — a so-called Rhineland bastard. And now you know why we cannot have children of our own. Now you know why we're here — to choose a child, someone we can love and protect.

(MRS. REYNOLDS heads for the back room. ANDRÉ stands while HEDDA sits, both in despairing silence.)

(MRS. REYNOLDS returns with the other album.)

MRS. REYNOLDS

I can't promise . . .

HEDDA

Thank you. . . . Oh, look, André.

(ANDRÉ and HEDDA begin to look through the two albums as the lights fade.)

(Fade out.)

The End

First We Have the Bris, Then We Eat the Brisket

Allan Yashin

Photo by Allan Yashin

Marsha hopes Aaron deals with a dire emergency before it's too late.

CHARACTERS

Aaron, nicely dressed, 30s
Marsha, his well-appointed wife, 30s.

TIME

Today

PLACE

Their well-furnished living room

(AARON and MARSHA are sitting in their living room.)

AARON

Gee, sweetheart, I can hardly wait. How many more weeks do you think it'll be?

MARSHA

Well, if I go full term it'll be another five weeks. But my mother said she gave birth to me three weeks early and that kind of thing can run in the family so —

AARON

So it might be only two weeks from now! Our little boy . . . oh sweetheart!

(AARON gives MARSHA a kiss.)

So that means my father was right!

MARSHA

About?

AARON

We can't wait any longer. We've got to hire the caterer for the bris now.

MARSHA

Caterer? What caterer? We're not getting married . . . we're just having a baby.

AARON

Just? We're *just* having a baby?

MARSHA

You know what I mean. We had 250 guests come to our wedding so of course we had to rent a hall and hire a caterer, but for a bris —

AARON

Well, we've got to invite the same 250 people to the bris, don't we? We don't want to insult anyone.

MARSHA

I see what this is about . . . it's your father. I've only got fifteen people in my whole family, but he's got to invite every relative in the phone book and every buyer he ever sold a shmatte to!

AARON

Shmattes! You didn't mind the money from his dress business paying for our wedding did you?

MARSHA

But a bris is a more intimate, private —

AARON

So, at my father's age you want to deprive him of the pleasure of —

MARSHA

Please . . . this arguing isn't good for the baby.

AARON

You're right, you're right . . . so I'll just call Moishe the caterer and put in our order for the day of the bris.

MARSHA

Alright, if it's so important to you. But we've still probably got over a month to go.

AARON

Sure, but that's a lot of meat. We've got to give him notice. If you figure a half a pound of brisket per person, that'll be 125 pounds, plus all the side dishes. And we gotta tell him the time of the day. Since first we have the bris and then we have the brisket, I'm figuring —

MARSHA

Wait a minute! We can't have the bris before the people eat.

AARON

Why not?

MARSHA

Because the last bris I went to that did that, my grandmother was weak from not eating and she got so upset about the whole circumcision business, that when she heard the baby cry, she passed out face first into the pickled herring fountain on the buffet table.

AARON

That's terrible! That fountain costs a fortune!

MARSHA

And when the moyl heard the splash, he spun around to see what happened. Everyone screamed because they thought he had cut the whole thing off. Grandma was so upset she wasn't able to eat all day after that. She had to lie on the couch with an icepack on her forehead and we had to talk in whispers the whole afternoon. So, no . . . we have to make sure the brisket is served before the bris!

AARON

Oh, so your grandmother is more important than thousands of years of tradition! And, besides, let me tell you about the time my Uncle Hesh went to a bris where they did serve the brisket first and he got so nauseous when he saw the moyl do his thing that he threw up into the punch bowl and —

MARSHA

Well, just because that Uncle Hesh of yours is too squeamish to . . . ooh . . . ooh . . . ooh . . .

AARON

What is it, what is it?

MARSHA

I'm feeling contractions, and they're strong!

AARON

Oh, no —

MARSHA

I feel like I'm going to be going into labor! You'd better call —

AARON

Yes, yes, of course, I'm dialing! Hello, hello! This is Aaron Feldman —

MARSHA

Tell them to hurry!

AARON

I am, I am! Yes, hello, It's Aaron Feldman of 42 First Avenue . . . it's an emergency! Moishe, I'm going to need 125 pounds of brisket by next week and you'd better throw in an extra ten gallons of pickled herring!

(Blackout)

The End

Shakes Hands

Milton Polsky

Photo by the UFT Players

An elderly Jewish merchant inspires
the Bard to write a play.

CHARACTERS

Will Shakespeare, early 40s
The Man, mid-70s
Offstage voices

TIME AND PLACE

A nice spring day, 1597, in the garden near the Globe Theater

(A beautiful spring morning in Southbank, London, 1597. WILL is writing at a table, scribbling in a tablet. A bearded older MAN, carrying a heavy bag, stops at the table. He is out of breath.)

WILL

You sound weary. I pray you, sit and rest a bit. Anything the matter?

MAN

(Putting down the bag and wiping his brow)

This madder is the matter.

WILL

Sir?

MAN

It's heavy here what came from the root of the madder, whose seeds sprout up shoots, their roots dug up and dried, ground to powder that makes a red dye, giving forth —

(Taking it out of the bag)

— this beautiful scarlet cloth that I hope to sell at the Spring Fair this day, thanks to the madder from which the red dye was made. Oh, but I do speak too long on't.

WILL

If you go on much longer, you'll make me madder than a madman in a Mummers' play wrestling a hobby horse —

MAN

I humbly apologize —

WILL

(Laughing)

No, you have a witty way with words, sir, that tickle me truly. I play with words too.

MAN

You do?

WILL

Yes. My curse. I call it divine annoyance. I'm a writer.

MAN

Ah, and you are writing now?

WILL

Yes, but only notes. While the theater is being built over there I enjoy writing in the garden here.

MAN

Notes? Ha, ha. But I hear not the sound of cornets flourishing in the air.

WILL

Now, sir, finally end to your puns. I fear tears of laughter will blot my paper.

(There is the sound of pounding coming from offstage.)

MAN

Words of any kind are better than that noise.

WILL

Oh, they're constructing a new theater over there, putting up the posts on blocks of cement to measure the land. The pounding is as hard on my ears as it on yours. Here, have an apple. The chewing may help.

(The MAN takes an apple, and a bite from it. The pounding stops.)
(Laughing)
See? Divine intervention.

(He takes another bite from his apple.)

MAN

Ah, a theater, you say, is being built over there?

WILL

The Theatre was the actual name of the old playhouse. The new one will be called the Globe. A touch-up o' modesty, don't you think, from just the theater to the whole world?

MAN

I've been away for five years now, so I have catching up to do. You write plays, then?

WILL

So they tell me. I've written a few. My last one concerned Henry the Fourth.

MAN

The fourth play?

WILL

No. I've actually written five or so now.

(He ponders and writes in his tablet.)

MAN

What's the new one about? Henry the Fifth?

WILL

No, about a merchant this time, m'thinks. From Venice, since my play will be about the business of commerce.

(Pounding again)

Ah, but nothing is sure when you start a new play. All I know is when we playwrights mean to build, we first survey — like that building over there — the plot.

MAN

A fair observation . . .

WILL

A line from my Henry the Fourth . . .

MAN

Well put.

WILL

Maybe, but I'm having a bit o' trouble plotting my new work . . . about the merchant.

MAN

Hmm. As you may sense, sir, I am one too — a merchant. From Florence. I daresay, the fairest city in the world producing thousands of yards of fine woolen cloth every day. That brings me back here to London, to sell what's in my woolsack at the Spring Fair here in Southbank.

WILL

Where our weavers are . . . fairly fine themselves, d'you think?

MAN

Oh, I beg to differ, sir! Our Italian cloth is much different, much better, because our weavers, I daresay, are stronger, pressing harder on their looms, thus making the weave so much closer —

(WILL rises, picks up his tablet, and dolefully looks at it for some seconds.) Anything the matter?

WILL

(Walking around, still looking at his notes in his tablet)
Yes, trying to weave my story strands together — the plot, the plot —

MAN

(Gets up)
Well, I must be moving on — I don't wish to disturb your thoughts —

WILL

No, stay. Perhaps you can help me straighten out some of my tangled strands.

(The MAN rises and offers his hand to WILL.)

MAN

I don't know how I . . . a Jew . . . can help you.

(WILL quickly withdraws his hand.)

WILL

Oh.

MAN

Surely you knew!

WILL

Well, I've never seen a Jew before.

MAN

(Sarcastically)
But certainly you saw my badge — the devil in disguise, so they say — or you smelled me, a cur, a loathsome dog. I cannot linger here. You'll faint from my execrable smell —

VOICE (O.S.)

Will! We need to run " Much Ado's" third scene — Come!

MAN

Will? William? Can it be you? William Shakespeare?!? Oh, I know who you are. Hath not a Jew ears to hear of your fame spread all the way to Italy?

WILL
As I said, I never met a Jew. I pray you, sit, sir.

(He does.)

MAN
Never — ?

WILL
Not in person. When I was but a lad in Stratford and a troupe of traveling players passed through, I saw a play with the character of a Jew in't, 'tis true. And five years ago, I saw the Jew Dr. Lopez hanged in the square for putting poison on our good queen's riding saddle — but even when they hanged him to the rafters, he denied being a Jew, so verily I still had not seen a Jew —

MAN
Aye, rubbish! Once born a Jew, one is always one, til the last dying day! Dr. Lopez, I assure you, died a Jew ev'n though denying it.

WILL
You may be right. Though, mark you, the crowd at his hanging, I recall, certainly didst scorn Dr. Lopez as a miserable Jew incarnate and hurled insults, even at his lifeless body —

MAN
And that is why I left England posthaste five years ago, when the hatred against my people was so vile that I could not stay another day after that hanging — on my last day here, I was spit on. Do you know how that feels? No, I suppose not.

(He takes a hard bite on his apple, spitting out some of it.)

WILL
Why did you come back now — There are not now many of your people here.

MAN
Why I return is my, shall we say, secret. Your plays have secrets, do they not?

WILL
Aye, they do. In this one, I'm thinking of having three trunks that hold a deep secret.

MAN
How can tree trunks hold secrets?

WILL

Not tree trunks, Signor Punster. Three . . . trunks — gold, silver, lead — a borrowing from Italian stories, signor —

MAN

Ah, pardon. This Jew's ears are hard of hearing. No matter, I mean secrets. Real secrets. The kind close to a person's heart. Real enough for it to be in your play.

WILL

Thank you, but I already have a merchant in my new work.

MAN

No, no, this merchant could be a Jew — perhaps someone who brokers a loan to the other merchant. What d' you call him?

WILL

Well, Antonio — tentative, mind you.

MAN

Tell me, what's the matter with him? What's his problem?

WILL

There's my problem, I don't know. I have no idea. I know he will seek justice, that's all.

MAN

Then why, pray tell, are you writing a play about a man you know nothing about? Except that he seeks justice? Come, we all seek that, sooner or later.

(The pounding starts again and then suddenly stops.)

WILL

The pounding again . . . Just when I need to think — I'm writing it because of the times, commerce, money, ships, I have an idea that this Antonio has ships and vouches for his best friend who needs money to court a certain lady — ask me not, don't know her name — anyway, the ships do not come back and he must pay for a loan he takes from — I'm stuck where my strands go all astray —

(Sound of pounding again)

There it is again. How many stakes do they have to pound in that hardened clay — *(Rising)* I hope the groundlings' hearts will pound as much when they see this play finished — if ever —

MAN

Master Will, an idea is glimmering. Perhaps this Antonio must pay a money lender, a userer with something close to his heart — a pound . . .

WILL

What — nails?

MAN

Nothing, nothing. Never mind, a trifle.

WILL

There was another story, too, I believe — something or the other about a pound — but it escapes me now — from Italy I believe.

MAN

Listen, Master Will, the man who gives the loan, you can make a . . . Jew.

WILL

I know nothing about them. I do know about usury. My father once made loans to some folk in Stratford — all honorable —

MAN

In Italy money lenders, no matter what they otherwise believe, are respected. I can help you to learn what you need to know about my fellow Hebrews.

WILL

You can?

VOICE (O.S.)

Will! We need to go over the "Much Ado" scene. Now!

WILL

(Calling)

Yes! Soon —

(Turning to the MAN, exasperatedly)

Actors. They have no patience.

(Inching up to the MAN.)

You can?

MAN

Yes. But you must help me. One strand ties another.

WILL

Help you? How so?

MAN

Do you recall when I offered you my hand and you refused to take it — Oh, I know, I know, what good Christian shakes hands with a lowly Jew? Well, when I extend my hand . . .

(He does that now.)

My hand is ringless, you see.

WILL

Yes, but —

MAN

Because my daughter ran off, in the middle of the night — with my ring — the very one my wife — God bless her soul — gave to me on our wedding night. My daughter did run off with my ring, five years ago — before I fled to Italy —

WILL

(Softly)

Your secret of the heart, I sense?

MAN

It is bad enough. To have a daughter run away from you . . . Never yours, I suppose.

WILL

No, I'm so so busy with my theater partners here, and with the writing and all — it often feels like I am running away from my daughters — even though I do manage to see them from time to time —

MAN

I haven't seen my daughter for five years! Oh, God, what did I do to deserve that!

(He lifts up his badge to reveal underneath it a torn black piece of cloth.)
She married and through her husband's power or spell, converted to a . . . Christian! In my eyes and by my faith she has betrayed our people — I will have no grandchild of our blood. Our ancient lingeage is dead. This is the shroud I wear — a black ribbon torn to shreds, as my heart is!

WILL

(Deeply moved)

I see, I see . . . And the way you hide it thus, that surely is your secret — I do not mean to intrude —

MAN

No, that is not my secret — the cut is deeper.

(Starts to get up)

Must go now — take my hand or not, I must go —

WILL

Your hand — ?

MAN

Oh, who cares if you shake it or not? Hands, eyes, ears, it's all surface, no special province of glittering gold . . . But to be accused of something that we do not have inside us or did not do. Oh, the injustice! Her husband, as do you all, believe my people did all those horrible things — seduce young boys, Christian boys, circumcise them, and drink their blood. To be accused of being cannibals! I implore you, put our outrage in your play! Truth and justice are what I seek.

WILL

Yes, but is that all? Speak, is there not something more?

MAN

Oh, you want something more? So you wish to dig up my secret like these workers dig up the ground of your new theater. Very well. And may the prophet Elijah carry what I tell you across the skies in fiery golden flames for all t' hear. I want her back, I want her back!

WILL

Yes . . . but you spok'st of how I could help you?

MAN

Come with me and talk to her. You have the words, you know what to say and when to say them — I want her back, not my ring — Surely in her heart she is still a Jew, like that Dr. Lopez was, and because she still must feel as a daughter to me — Come with me now and shine a good deed in my darkest world.

WILL

. . . Yes, 'twould be well to speak with her.

MAN

But then what if her husband —

WILL

Arrange to meet her somewhere then. Here if you like . . .

VOICE (O.S.)

Will, stop writing for a minute! Damn!! We'll do the scene without you if you don't come now! We'll make changes without you!

WILL

I have to go, it will not do to upset my actors — will you return here with her?

(Starts to go)

MAN

Why? To put me on trial . . . ?

WILL

(Coming back)

No, no — to talk — together —

MAN

Talk? So that your players rehearsing in the garden back there can hear all and jeer at the old man and his apostate errant daughter sparring while ev'ryone has a hearty laugh and spit on me again . . . No thank you!

WILL

Not in my thoughts at all — Just us!

MAN

So you could put it all into your play, I'll wager. Oh, so clever of you —

WILL

Come, thou mistak'st me. In good faith, m'thought we might all talk, that is all.

VOICE

Will, you're taking longer than a Jews — beard!!

(Silence. The MAN rises, picks up his woolsack.)

WILL

No, stay —

(He rises, faces direction of the theater.)

I'll —

MAN

No.

(Covering his hurt, laughs softly.)

Jews — beard . . . O, what's in a name, eh?

MAN (Cont'd)

(Sinking back in the bench, a long pause)
Talk? No, what use would be? Words, words, words! No, after five years, no pleading words of mine, or even yours, would change her. You'll never understand what I feel, what I really want.

WILL

But why, if not for her, did you came back here?

MAN

Yes . . . I know, but never mind that now — I will go back to Italy — right after the fair — I won't see her, now or forever — !

WILL

Wait, hear me now — might she not be like Dr. Lopez, faithful inside. A feeling inside of still being a Jew? How would you know if you don't talk with her yourself, heart to heart, and hear what she has to say — ?

MAN

Yes, that may be what I should do . . . But no, her Christian husband would only bar my way . . .
(Sighs)
If only he were just a bit like you . . . if only . . . If . . .
(Pauses, close to tears)

WILL

May none e'er deprive us of that dream of "if" . . . Old man, I truly understand thy pain. I wish thee well.

(He extends his hand.)

MAN

(Taking it)
And you, with my blessings . . .

(They shake hands warmly.)

Though I am still most troubled o'er my family loss, my heart now has been lightened. You have just showed me how this land might be from the narrow and grudging world I fled from.

WILL

(Softly)
Change?

MAN

O, but I pray it will, sir, when I find men such as you, who will shake the hand of one like me . . . who has other . . . other . . . outside leanings.

WILL

I fear not all men here may act thus like me.

VOICE (O.S.)

Master Will, we wait for you to join us!

MAN

Well, my good friend, I look forward to the time when I may return to see your true and caring play about the merchant . . . mayhaps with her . . .

WILL

(Picking up his tablet, shrugs)
For now, farewell, and go in peace.

(The MAN bows respectfully and exits. WILL shakes head, gazing after departed MAN.)

Pray, do not come to see my play, if I were t'write it, for it can be neither true or caring, nor can it show the glow that warms my heart for thee. Alas, poor friend, this bright land loves thee not, nor mayhaps ev'n me, if they but knew that I befriended thee — one who keeps outside our common ways.

VOICE (O.S.)

Master Will, come down — come down to see us play this scene — else you miss all your merriment!

WILL

(Aside, glumly)
Yes, my merriment . . . Ah, thou fine wool — dealer, you have shown me the web of life — a tangled yarn of good and ill together. (Calls) I come, I come . .

(His eyes downcast, he goes off.)

(Slow fadeout)

The End

A Chance Encounter

Milton Polsky

Photo by Andrew Benjamin

Emile and Donna share a small space and a large difference of opinions.

CHARACTERS

Donna Atkins, American, in work clothes, 20s
Emile Rackaus, American, German descent, in work clothes, 30s

TIME

A late afternoon in July, 1936

PLACE

A little storeroom at the Astoria Pool in Astoria, Queens. Small table. Several T-shirts are hung up. Some brooms, mops and pails are visible in the corner. Sheets of colored papers on the wall. The door facing the offstage pool deck is fully open.

EMILE

(He comes in with a sketchbook, puts it in corner then picks up mop, stands next to DONNA)

So glad I could step in to help you . . . with the final two heats to go . . . How can I help?

DONNA

You know how to swab down the water after each race?

EMILE

Sure . . . I worked in the diving pool in the morning . . . The heat's — how do you say — getting to us…a joke…Okay, okay, I'll do the mopping up . . . My last day here anyway, so I'll do a good job . . . it's beginning to get dark — getting close to closing, good, huh?

DONNA

(Looking out of open door to pool deck)

I guess . . . How'd you come to this country anyway? I mean. if you don't mind me —

EMILE

No, not at all. My brother was sick here in Astoria, so I come to visit, from Austria — five years ago and stayed.

DONNA

What did he have?

EMILE

Pneumonia . . .

DONNA

How's he doing?

EMILE

I was by his side til he passed.

DONNA

Sorry, I know how that is . . . I'm studying to be a nurse.

EMILE

Very good. He was a good man. His lungs gave out. No wonder, the place where he lived, that whole section in Astoria, is run-down, polluted . . .

DONNA

Sorry . . .

EMILE

I'm supposed to paint murals on park and playground walls around here—and community center walls — how did I end up here? — mopping up sweaty water from pool decks — Moving from park to park with pools like this. Funny, huh? I'm an artist! Went to the Art Students League . . . in Manhattan.

DONNA

Well, we have to do what we have to do . . . I work late nights in a hospital.
(SOUND of loud clapping and cheering)

VOICE (O.S.)

(BOOMING)
It's a close competition, folks! Get ready for the final two races of the American women's swimming trials for the 1936 Olympics coming up in Berlin . . . Men's trials here tomorrow . . . Thank you for coming to Astoria, Queens, New York, USA!

DONNA

You can go out there . . . need help?

(He shakes his head, moves off with the mop. She looks around, spots his sketchbook on the table and curiously leafs through it.)

(SOUND of clapping, Cheers. "Great, Kathy! Attaway to go," etc. After a minute, he returns from pool deck.)

DONNA

That was fast.

EMILE

(Looking out to pool from of open door)
I told you I was an artist, so I'm handy with a brush, ha! . . . I just whisk-away!

DONNA

I didn't mean you . . . her time — terrific! Mind if I look at some of your work?

(He gives her the okay. EMILE smiles as DONNA leafs through his sketchbook.)

VOICE

(BOOMING)
Katherine Louise Rawlings, 19, from Nashville, Tennessee qualifies for the 100-meter sprint. One minute, four and six tenths seconds! Yes! Congratulations, Kathy, from the Tennessee Valley to the New York Harbor!

DONNA

Who's the last picture of — the man with the little mustache. Your brother?

EMILE

Not finished yet with it . . . No, the chancellor of Germany. He, too, was an artist, a darn good one. You know, he's Austrian, where I'm from.

DONNA

No, I didn't know that . . . Uh-huh, so, you're a darn good artist, too —

EMILE

Maybe . . . But he's the amazing one. I assume, then, you don't know all he did — swept into the Rhineland last year, with great popular success. And some day, he will take over Austria, which is fine with us — and I will be there waiting for him. He did something else last year, too, terrific—
(Starts sketching)

DONNA

(Laughing)
Can't wait to see what you've done — but shake a leg, hurry — next race comin' up . . . Doing my good side, Emile?

EMILE

Ach! So you know my name —

DONNA

(Motioning toward his sketchbook)
Mine's Donna . . . Nice to meet you.

EMILE

(Bowing politely)
Well, Donna, too bad I am assigned here at the Astoria Pool for only one day . . .

(Taking a step toward her)

DONNA

(Moving a step away from him)

Too bad you won't see 'em tomorrow. Men's trials. So what's the thing you wanted to tell me?

EMILE

When?

DONNA

(Starting to sweep floor)
Before you started drawing me again . . .

EMILE

Oh, yeah . . . about Heinrich Himmler, the chancellor's right-hand man . . . word's going around he started a remarkable new program . . . Lebensborn . . . to raise babies to be special to serve the New Reich . . .

DONNA

(Stops sweeping)
Babies — ?

EMILE

Ja, little ones, to receive special attention to, how you say, fulfill the Aryan dream of idealized perfection . . .

DONNA

You jokin' again? No one starts that way as babies . . . those top swimmers out there didn't start out that way . . .

EMILE

This is different. The Chancellor has dreams, and the will to pursue them.

DONNA

. . . Idealized perfection? Is that eugenics? C'mon, my pediatrics professor at Mount Sinai Hospital . . . Dr. Stein she mentioned that . . . but she scoffed at the idea — we talked about it in class, but I don't know . . . it doesn't seem ethically right to me, or fair to make that national policy. Even if it were the right thing to do — what would you get, blue-eyed robots?

(SOUND: Clapping and cheers from outside. She looks at the sketch EMILE is drawing.)

DONNA

This little drawing you did of me. You made me a blonde? And you shortened my nose. That's not me. You trying out your ideology on me?

VOICE (O.S)

(Over clapping)

Great heat, folks! Another terrific time for . . .

(VOICE trails off. DONNA goes off to the pool with a mop. EMILE closes the door.)

EMILE

(He works on her drawing some more, singing to himself. After a bit, she returns.)

Hey, Donna . . .You know, you're pretty quick, too.

DONNA

Well, you have to be fast, too, to work in the emergency room.

EMILE

(Showing her the sketchbook again)

Yes . . . Take a look at these pages — I managed to make a few quick sketches of the swimmers on my lunch hour. As you see, they are quite lovely, eh?

DONNA

Oh, but they all look alike — blonde, good figures, tall . . . Didn't you notice, we have black athletes on the team, too?

EMILE

Ah, yes . . .You Americans especially seem to adore the track star, Jesse someone — I don't think my chancellor will shake hands with him if he wins . . . I told you, he has integrity, my chancellor does.

DONNA

Don't go blowin' your wig, Emile. You said he likes special babies, the kind that will grow into white superstars . . . One thing: You never told me where those hot-shot babies are coming from.

EMILE

(Rhapsodic)

Where they come from you ask? — Like the Nordic gods they will become, they dropped from the heavens onto Atlantis in the Northland — from our healthiest Aryan specimens. Your darling Mr. Roosevelt would not think of doing that. Well, what do you expect from a —

(He whispers into her ear. She recoils.)

DONNA

So now Roosevelt is Jewish . . . Damn!! You really like making things up, don't you, yeah, like turning this swimming meet into some kind of super race that stinkin' sketchbook of yours!

EMILE

No, you look at the facts! Roosevelt hides his true identity! Pretending to be one of us! He's from New York, isn't he? Where all of them live? Anyway, no imagination, like our chancellor. What does Roosevelt do for his people? Fixes roads, puts on plays, paints walls on community centers . . . Why doesn't he fix up places like where my brother lived — if you call it that . . . No, the president is just —

DONNA

Oh, shut up! I got this job — so did you — through his plans of putting people to work!

EMILE

As what, a janitor? Instead of painting wall murals or showing my real talent as an artist? My chancellor wouldn't do that . . . so I look forward to the day when I can leave Astoria for Austria and then to do what I can to serve my chancellor—

DONNA

CHANCELLOR THIS AND CHANCELLOR THAT! *(Recovering, clapping hands)* Bravo, bravo — just go home. Go home —

(Picks up sketchbook from the table, walks over to him)

EMILE

(Taking sketchbook. Quietly)

Yes, leave your beloved Astoria. Did you know? — named after a German immigrant, America's first millionaire! He had some . . . you know, in his bloodline . . . My brother said it was a little village here once, then became a resort for the high and mighty ferried over from Manhattan . . . Since then, became polluted by hoards of poverty-stricken immigrants . . .

DONNA

People trying to fix things up! Well, you don't have to stay here! Astoria won't miss you, believe me — and take your bull about pretty robots with you!

EMILE

Okay, okay. I will soon return to Austria and wait for our . . . our fuehrer . . .

EMILE (Cont'd)

to enter our borders. I will serve him in peace and, of course, in war, if that comes.

(Pauses)

Well, I guess I have done my work for the day. Nice meeting you . . .

(Bows)

Auf wiedersehen.

DONNA

Sorry about your brother. Goodbye!

(A small laugh)

And that would be something . . . If we did meet again . . . somewhere on some battlefield — you fighting for your new country— and as a nurse, me fighting for mine.

(EMILE extends his hand. She pauses, does not take it. He heads out, sketchbook in hand. She slowly returns the mop to corner.)

VOICE

That's it, folks, for today. Hurry back tomorrow for the American Men's Qualifiers for the Olympics in Berlin this summer. Remember, everyone here is a champion! Be careful on your way out.

(DONNA pauses, looks around room, and exits.)

(Blackout)

The End

(Production note: The last minute might be staged in a way so it is left to the audience to discern whether or not DONNA shakes EMILE'S hand.)

I Feel Their Pain

Allan Yashin

Photo by: Andrew Benjamin

Morris needs Cynthia's help during Occupy Wall Street.

CHARACTERS

Morris, 60s
Cynthia, his wife, 60s

TIME

Evening, September, 2011

PLACE

The well-appointed living room of their apartment in lower Manhattan

(CYNTHIA, smartly dressed, sits reading a copy of *Psychology Today*. A VOICE is heard coming from another part of the apartment.)

MORRIS (O.S.)
Cynthia, please, I need your help!

CYNTHIA
I'm just finishing this article in *Psychology Today*, Morris. What is it?

MORRIS (O.S.)
Would you help me find the front door?

CYNTHIA
Find the front door? It's the same place it's been in for the past thirty years. What're you talking about?

(MORRIS stumbles into the living room wearing a blindfold.)

Oh, my goodness . . . just what are you doing with that blindfold on? Are you going to a Pin the Tail on the Donkey tournament?

MORRIS
Please, this isn't the time for an attempt at humor. Just lead me to the elevator . . . the doorman will help me from there.

CYNTHIA
Morris, have you finally flipped your lid? I told you to call your doctor to increase the dosage on your medication!

MORRIS
Cynthia, my lid is firmly attached to the top of my head where it belongs. I only wish my problem could be ameliorated by more medication, but it can't.

CYNTHIA
(Sighing, but attempting to be patient)
What problem can you possibly have that can be helped by making a complete fool of yourself?

MORRIS
What problem! What problem! What else . . . the economy! Every program on NPR, PBS, CNN, MSNBC, or — shudder to say it — the FOX network . . . that's all they talk about.The pundits try to outdo themselves with apocalyptic scenarios.

CYNTHIA

You're absolutely right about that . . . but it still doesn't explain why you're wearing . . .

(CYNTHIA points to his blindfold.)

MORRIS

(Whipping off the blindfold)

Prospects have never seemed bleaker, Cynthia, can't you see that? Each time I look at a newspaper the news gets worse. Headlines screaming layoffs . . . foreclosures . . . pension givebacks . . . college grads with no job prospects and unpayable student loans . . . the financial crisis charting ever upward while the Congressional meltdown has the economy on its knees.

CYNTHIA

Very aptly put, Morris . . . but wouldn't a letter to the *New York Times* editorial page be a better way to express your concern than wandering around with a blindfold?

MORRIS

Oh, you think so! Then tell me just one thing . . . have you looked out that window?

CYNTHIA

Why, is there anyone standing on the ledge?

MORRIS

Sarcasm in the face of the abyss . . . it's not an attractive trait, Cynthia. Not when I see the formerly employed wondering aimlessly through the streets, wondering where their next meal is coming from. Old pensioners forced out of their apartments and living in refrigerator crates along the river. Protesters camping out in parks to vent their frustration at the inequalities of our economic system. I just can't bear the sight of all that suffering anymore!

CYNTHIA

Wait a second . . . now I remember! We used to play that game where I put on my negligee and you wore a blindfold and tried to catch me as I ran around the bedroom! That's the same blindfold isn't it? Come on . . . isn't it?

MORRIS

That may be the case, but it doesn't change the fact that —

CYNTHIA
And if you caught me, I would have to do . . . you know what. But if I got away, then you would have to —

MORRIS
Fond memories, Cynthia . . . I'm not denying it . . . but there's a world full of strife out there and —

CYNTHIA
I can put on my negligee and get your mind off all that strife . . . and I'll let you catch me this time.

MORRIS
But . . . but . . . I feel their pain!

CYNTHIA
Then take two Percocets and come to bed.

(CYNTHIA gives him a beckoning seductive look and points towards the bedroom.)

MORRIS
It's a tempting offer . . . but I'm going out there!

(MORRIS puts on the blindfold again and begins to slowly grope his way towards the door.)

So if you have any compassion for me you'll help me get to the elevator.

CYNTHIA
And just where are you planning to go with that blindfold anyway?

MORRIS
To Duane Reade to buy a pair of earplugs so I can't hear the heartbreaking moan of the masses anymore.

(CYNTHIA goes over to MORRIS and pulls off the blindfold.)

Cynthia, what are you doing?

CYNTHIA
I'm not letting you go out there without me! If you're so attuned to the pain of the masses then why don't we both get a closer look at the occupation? Maybe

we can do some good.

MORRIS

It wouldn't be the first time we found ourselves part of a large protest movement. Do you remember?

CYNTHIA

Yes, yes . . . the peace demonstrations in Central Park in the '60s! Of course, that was the day we . . .

MORRIS

That's right, dear; it was the day we met. There were tens of thousands in the Great Meadow protesting against the war, listening to those impassioned speeches and chanting — We Want Peace and We Want it Now!

CYNTHIA

Power to the People!

MORRIS

Hell, No, We Won't Go!

CYNTHIA

I saw you there in the crowd wearing your love beads and holding a sign that said, "We Won't Get Fooled Again!" and I think I fell in love on the spot.

MORRIS

And with your long paisley skirt and flowers in your hair and your face beaming, I thought you were the most beautiful girl in the crowd.

CYNTHIA

I remember when the rally was breaking up we were so filled with the excitement of being fiercely committed to a cause —

MORRIS

The way the 99 percent in the park outside are committed.

CYNTHIA

— that we didn't want to leave Central Park. We wanted to revel in the feeling that we had accomplished something very important that day.

MORRIS

And revel we did my darling! Revel we did! Do you remember?

CYNTHIA
It must've been those joints they were passing around in the crowd.

MORRIS
You know what we heard Abbie Hoffman say? "A rally without pot is like a seder without matzo."

CYNTHIA
I haven't thought of what we did that night in ages!

MORRIS
You haven't? Why I think of it all the time . . . you little temptress. When you were carrying a sign that said "Make Love, Not War" . . . what do you expect to happen?

CYNTHIA
Stop, Morris . . . . I'm blushing after forty years. I can't believe you talked me into making love right there in Central Park . . . within sight of all those mounted policemen.

MORRIS
They weren't the only ones mounted that night.

CYNTHIA
Morris, you're embarrassing me . . .

MORRIS
Our emotions were enflamed . . . Demonstration and disobedience in the name of world peace. It's a heady brew! The next thing we knew we were crawling through the bushes looking for a private place to consecrate our commitment to the movement.

CYNTHIA
Oh, Morris, you still have your wonderful way with words. I think that's what convinced me to do it that night in Central Park.

MORRIS
Then come out to the park with me right now to join the 99 percenters! Let us renew our commitment to fight inequality where ever we find it!

CYNTHIA
But it's dark now and the protests have ended for the day.

MORRIS

That's exactly the right time for the demonstration I have in mind . . . and there are plenty of bushes in the park.

CYNTHIA

What're you talking about?

MORRIS

It's a once-in-a-lifetime opportunity to recapture the fervor of our youth. Our lovemaking will be a protest against corporate greed and government gridlock!

CYNTHIA

Have you lost your mind?

MORRIS

Well, a minute ago you said you were ready to put on your negligee.

CYNTHIA

That was in the privacy of my own bedroom . . . not on Wall Street. And besides, you'd end up getting us arrested in about two minutes.

MORRIS

So much the better! We'd end up as heroes . . . seniors using their sexuality to express their dedication to fight social inequality after thirty years of marriage!

CYNTHIA

Please calm down, Morris.

MORRIS

We'll be media darlings . . . Oprah will book us for a full sixty minutes . . . We'll be on Barbara Walter's list of the ten most fascinating people . . . Dr. Oz will want to examine us on network TV . . . We'll be the AARP Couple of the Year!

CYNTHIA

I don't want to burst your little bubble of self-aggrandizement . . . but you're not exactly the man you were back in the '60s in Central Park.

MORRIS

And just what is that supposed to mean?

CYNTHIA

Well . . . you've developed a few . . . deficiencies.

MORRIS

That's not very sensitive of you to bring it up.

CYNTHIA

Bringing it up isn't the problem . . . keeping it up, is.

MORRIS

Don't worry about that . . . I'll take one of my little wonder pills.

CYNTHIA

It's not just that . . . it's also your back. I can hardly see you crawling around through the bushes and using the hard ground for a mattress.

MORRIS

You underestimate me, Cynthia . . . I'm still as agile as a cat. Just look!

(MORRIS drops to the floor and starts to crawl on all fours.)

See . . . see, I'm still the same man I was!

(MORRIS looks over his shoulder to talk to CYNTHIA as he crawls.)

Come on down here and join . . . Aargh! Aargh! My back! My back!

CYNTHIA

(Rushing over to help MORRIS up)

I've got you, dear, I've got you! There, let me help you up.

MORRIS

(Slowly getting up and walking bent over in pain)

Help me get to the chair. Do you have those Percocets?

(CYNTHIA helps MORRIS gingerly sit down.)

CYNTHIA

I feel your pain, dear, but there goes our night of passion in the bushes. I'll call up Oprah's people and cancel the interview.

MORRIS

I'm sorry, Cynthia . . . you were right. I guess I'm not the man I used to be.

CYNTHIA

(Touching MORRIS's face affectionately)

In my eyes, I still see you wearing those love beads.

MORRIS

Thanks, sweetheart . . . but now it's up to you. You've got to go out to the park to represent both of us.

CYNTHIA

What . . . what do you mean?

MORRIS

All those young people need the guidance of someone who went through the civil rights and peace movements in the '60s. Back then we worried about the oppressed minority but now we're worrying about the exploited majority. Whatever happened to the assumption that each generation would do better than the one that came before? The world is spinning backwards on its axis!

CYNTHIA

But what do you want me to do?

MORRIS

Just give all those young people your support. Tell them that in the '60s it was people just like them that helped change the world to a better place. Would you do that for me, darling?

CYNTHIA

(Getting on her coat and walking towards the door)

Yes, yes, I will. You're the same good man you've always been . . . I'll tell them that too.

MORRIS

And tell them the protest needs a clearly defined agenda . . . goals to coalesce around legislative policy.

CYNTHIA

(Calling back to him as she stands at the front door)

I will . . . I will.

MORRIS

Tell them Morris is 100% behind the 99%! And Cynthia . . . Cynthia . . . one more important thing! Stay out of those damned bushes!

CYNTHIA

Well, if you're so worried about that, why don't you come with me?

MORRIS

All right, I will!

(Slowly getting up and walking towards CYNTHIA)

I'm coming, I'm coming. Aargh!! I feel my pain!

(Lights fade to black.)

The End

A Stroll in the Garden

Milton Polsky

Photo by George Miller Associates

What will a famous impresario think of Sarah's singing?

CHARACTERS

Hava Margolis, a college professor, about 50
Becky Parness, a high school teacher, 45
Sarah Goldstein, their mother, who has Alzheimer's Disease, 80
Sir Rudolf Bing, an impresario, former General Manager, Metropolitan Opera Company, also has Alzheimer's Disease, 80
Janet Reynolds, his private nurse, 40

TIME

Around noon, on a Sunday April, 1989

PLACE

The garden of the Hebrew Home for the Aged in Riverdale, New York

(HAVA and BECKY are with their mother, Sarah, sitting on a bench in the garden.)

HAVA

Look there, the buds are opening up. I love those daffodils. This garden is so refreshing.

BECKY

I think we should head back inside. It's going to rain.

HAVA

Just one more breath of fresh air . . .

BECKY

Mom, it's time for lunch. They got your favorite . . . corned beef and cabbage.

SARAH

Is it lean at least? Guten's always cuts lean.

BECKY

Hava and I are visiting you today. It's time for lunch.

SARAH

Corned beef? We going to Guten Brothers or Cohen's?

HAVA

Those two delis are in Milwaukee, Mom. Remember, we could never make up our minds on Sunday which one to go to.

BECKY

Let's go inside, Hava . . . I'm starving.

HAVA

Thinking about yourself . . . Mom should have a salad instead of fatty corned beef.

BECKY

She enjoys the corned beef.

HAVA

I'm not going to argue you with you, sis. You think you know best, go for it.

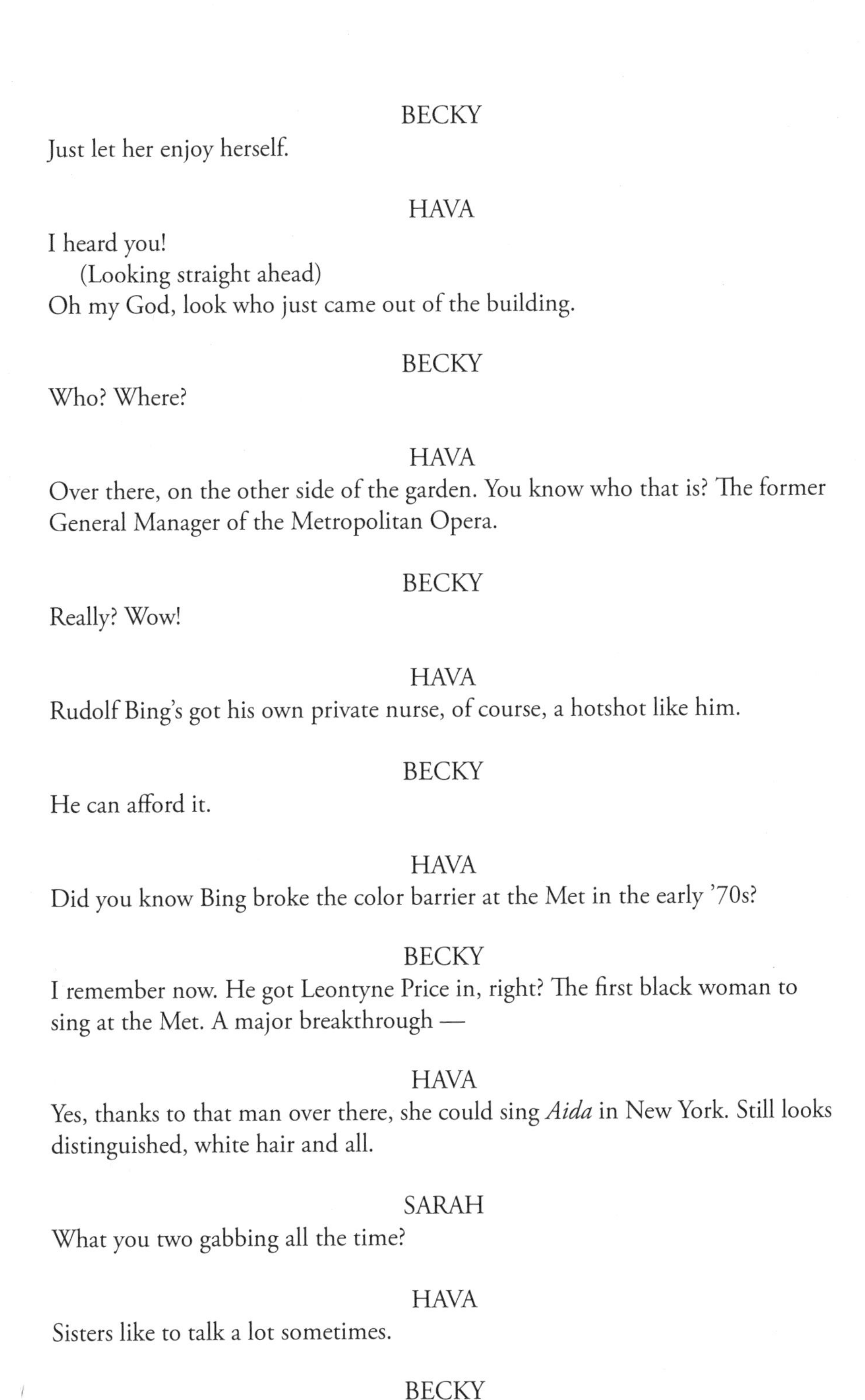

BECKY

Just let her enjoy herself.

HAVA

I heard you!
(Looking straight ahead)
Oh my God, look who just came out of the building.

BECKY

Who? Where?

HAVA

Over there, on the other side of the garden. You know who that is? The former General Manager of the Metropolitan Opera.

BECKY

Really? Wow!

HAVA

Rudolf Bing's got his own private nurse, of course, a hotshot like him.

BECKY

He can afford it.

HAVA

Did you know Bing broke the color barrier at the Met in the early '70s?

BECKY

I remember now. He got Leontyne Price in, right? The first black woman to sing at the Met. A major breakthrough —

HAVA

Yes, thanks to that man over there, she could sing *Aida* in New York. Still looks distinguished, white hair and all.

SARAH

What you two gabbing all the time?

HAVA

Sisters like to talk a lot sometimes.

BECKY

It keeps us in touch, Mom.

SARAH

That's good.

HAVA

Mom, we just saw a man who used to run the Met. He's a knight. Sir Rudolf Bing.

SARAH

What?

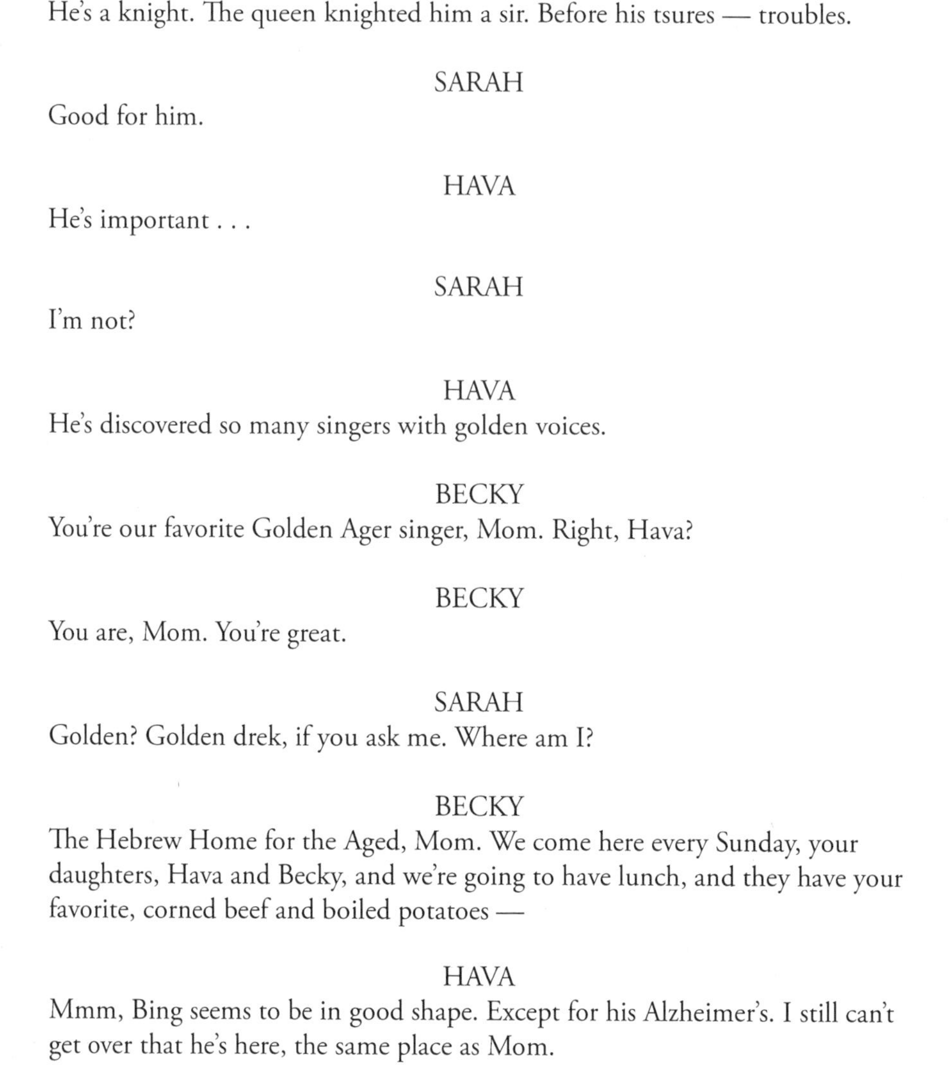

HAVA

He's a knight. The queen knighted him a sir. Before his tsures — troubles.

SARAH

Good for him.

HAVA

He's important . . .

SARAH

I'm not?

HAVA

He's discovered so many singers with golden voices.

BECKY

You're our favorite Golden Ager singer, Mom. Right, Hava?

BECKY

You are, Mom. You're great.

SARAH

Golden? Golden drek, if you ask me. Where am I?

BECKY

The Hebrew Home for the Aged, Mom. We come here every Sunday, your daughters, Hava and Becky, and we're going to have lunch, and they have your favorite, corned beef and boiled potatoes —

HAVA

Mmm, Bing seems to be in good shape. Except for his Alzheimer's. I still can't get over that he's here, the same place as Mom.

BECKY

He's lucky . . . C'mon, we'll talk about it at lunch.

HAVA

I don't know, but wouldn't it be a hoot if . . .

BECKY

If — ?

HAVA

If Mom could sing a song . . . a Yiddish song for Sir Rudolf?

BECKY

To him? Are you kidding? C'mon, let's go in —

HAVA

You are one antsy woman, Sis. I think Mom would enjoy that.

BECKY

Please, don't. It's not a good idea.

HAVA

Why not?

BECKY

Why? So you can tell your friends that your mother sang for the great impresario of the Metropolitan Opera?

HAVA

No, I think she would enjoy doing it, isn't that enough?

BECKY

How on Earth can she, if she can't understand what she's doing? What if she calls him Dad, or someone, embarrassing, where's the enjoyment in that?

HAVA

She would, she would enjoy it. She knows things we don't think she does. You know that.

BECKY

You would enjoy it!

HAVA

It has nothing to do with me . . . It's music. Expression. In the moment. It would be nice. Because she doesn't understand something doesn't mean she can't enjoy it. She enjoys a good corned beef sandwich. Well, her singing is nourishment too. It doesn't matter who she sings for.

BECKY

I don't agree. Bing is different. He's . . .

HAVA

A man who enjoys music, singing. That should be enough. Let her sing with Bing or with whomever — it don't mean a thing . . . if you don't got that zing. She has it whether she knows it or not. She feels . . .

SARAH

You two, stop it!

HAVA

Mom, would you like to sing a song now for that man over there? I think he would love to hear you sing a nice, Yiddish song — "Belz," "Paparosin" — one of the songs you like to sing here in the Hebrew Home chorus . . . He's a good man. . . I think . . .

(A silence)

SARAH

Sing? Okay. I thought we were going to Gutens on North Avenue. I love the smell of the sausages hanging from the ceiling. I love the dust, what do you call it, the sawdust on the floor. I love all their stuff — the smell of that pastrami . . .

BECKY

Yes, Mom.

SARAH

Yeah, that's it. Pastrami, okay, Jake, you take out the Dodge from the garage and pick up some good things at Guten's. It's Sunday, a nice day — be careful. You take it easy with the car, you hear?

(Pointing to BING, coming closer to them)

Who's the man? Jake? Jake, that you?

HAVA

He's not Pa, Mom. His name is Rudolf Bing. He's a famous man who was with the Metropolitan Opera House. He's nice, like Pa was. You feel like singing now? You can sing to Pa.

(BING and JANET are at their side now.)

Ah, Mr. Bing, so nice to meet you, Sir. And you, Ma'am. This is my sister Becky and mother Sarah Goldstein. She came over from Russia when she was 13, and worked in a factory making stockings. We all lived in Milwaukee. She also sang songs for Jewish charities at events like the City of Hope Foundation and Pioneer Women. When my dad died, she went to live in Miami Beach and sang songs right on the beach there on Ninth Street.

(HAVA walks quickly over to BING and JANET, who are sitting on the bench.)

Everyone loved it and her — and she sings in the Hebrew Home chorus here . . . Would you like to hear her sing something now? I'm sure she would enjoy that . . . and you too, Sir Rudolf.

(BING just stands there, smiling.)

JANET

Sure, he would. Go ahead, Mrs. Goldstein. Sing a song, a Yiddish song, if you would like. I've heard you in one of the talent shows here . . . You sing nice.

BECKY

It's okay, Mom. Sing a song for Mr. Bing. Or for Pa . . .

(SARAH nods yes. As she is about to sing, HAVA takes out her camera to take a picture of SARAH and BING, who are standing together. But JANET shakes her head not to do that. BECKY seems embarrassed.)

BECKY

No, Hava . . .

(HAVA pauses and puts the camera away.)

I feel some drops.

JANET

Just a sunshower. You can use our umbrella.

(JANET opens her umbrella and gently places SARAH and BING under it. SARAH sings the Yiddish song for BING, who is smiling.)

Thank you, Mrs. Goldstein. Mr. Bing thanks you. You made him so happy.

BING

Thank you.

JANET

Good luck with all your singing. My, it looks like it stopped raining. Hmm, that was a short shpritz, as you say. Just a sunshower.
(BING gently shakes SARAH's hand. JANET and BING head the other way and BECKY and HAVA face each other.)

HAVA

Thanks, Becky . . .

(The sisters kiss each other, then hold SARAH's hand gently, as they all continue to walk as the lights fade out.)

The End

Mister Mitzvah Maker

Allan Yashin

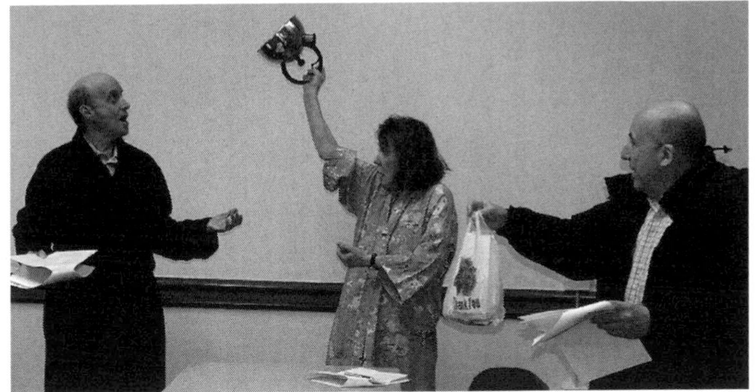

Photo by Andrew Benjamin

An unexpected greeting for an unexpected guest.

CHARACTERS

Samuel, 60s
Agnes, Samuel's wife, 60s
Sarah, their daughter, 20s
Fanuel, a mysterious stranger, 30-40s

TIME

Today

PLACE

The dining room of a modest apartment

AGNES

(She enters stretching and yawning, wearing a bathrobe. Troubled.)
Oy, oy, oy, Samuel, it's 7:30 on a Sunday morning and you're out already. What am I going to do with you? God knows what crazy business you're up to now?

(Sitting at the dining room table, she notices a sheet of paper, picks it up, and reads it.)

"If you're reading this note I hope you're not too hungry yet. I'll be back with your breakfast soon. You can eat in bed if you want to. Samuel."
(Wistfully)
Ah, . . . he thinks of going out to get me breakfast and serving me in bed. And look, he signs his name, as if I wasn't married to him for forty-three years. Ah, Samuel, you don't have to buy me breakfast. It's not going to do much good.

(Door to second bedroom swings open, and unseen by AGNES, a young scruffy-looking man wearing a bathrobe enters the room.)

FANUEL

Are the bagels here yet?

AGNES

(Turning to see the man standing there, then screaming in shock)
Yaaa! Who are you?! Who are you?!

FANUEL

(Stepping closer to AGNES)
I heard you talking about breakfast so —

AGNES

Stay away from me! Stay away from me!

FANUEL

Stop screaming! I don't like screaming!

AGNES

(Runs to sink, grabs a pot, which she brandishes like a weapon)
Get out of here before I slam you in the head with this —

(Front door swings open and SAMUEL comes in, carrying a big paper bag.)

SAMUEL

Oh, good, I see you two have met. I've got the bagels.

AGNES

What?!

SAMUEL

(Pointing to the pot AGNES is still holding)

I see you're going to boil water for coffee. Good! Good!

FANUEL

You're making instant right? Right? Regular gets on my nerves!

SAMUEL

Don't worry, didn't I tell you Agnes makes a great cup of coffee?

AGNES

What is going on here?!

SAMUEL

Wait, Agnes, wait! Fanuel must be starving.

AGNES

Oh, excuse me! Daniel is starving.

(Holding up the note)

And here I was silly enough to think you were actually getting breakfast for me.

SAMUEL

It's Fanuel, not Daniel.

(Taking bagels out of bag)

I got you lox on an everything bagel. You like that, Fanuel?

FANUEL

(Taking the bagel)

And no onions. Good, they don't like onions upstairs.

(He starts to enter the bedroom with the bagel, then stops.)

Good . . . but not good enough.

(He enters the bedroom.)

AGNES

Who is that ungrateful shnorrer? You give him a bagel and lox, but it's not good enough? Let him go upstairs where they don't like onions if it's not good enough.

SAMUEL

Please! He'll hear you.

AGNES

God forbid, I should hurt his feelings, Fanuel, Shmanuel, whoever he is!

SAMUEL

You don't understand. He's had a very difficult life. I found him sleeping on a park bench last night while I was out for my jog, and I brought him up here while you were asleep.

(He grabs a notebook and starts to write in it as he talks to himself.)

One a.m. . . . found Fanuel in Riverside Park . . . gave him shelter . . . bought bagels and lox . . .

AGNES

You promised me you would stop this after you gave the 70th-birthday present I gave you to that man who stands outside the subway station begging for change.

SAMUEL

That's right! I nearly forgot about that one.
(Writing in the notebook)
Gave new gold Jewish star to needy man at 75th Street subway stop.

AGNES

And don't forget your last Social Security check. You sent it to that Jewish tribe in Mozambique so they could fly in a rabbi for a bar mitzvah.

SAMUEL

That I did not forget. It's here on page one, just after the thousand dollars I sent to the church in St. Petersburg to help repair stained-glass windows.

AGNES

God, to a church?!?

SAMUEL

And yesterday I packed all the old sandals and flip flops we had laying around the closet and sent 'em to a Buddhist temple in Myanmar.

AGNES

Bar mitzvahs in Africa! Churches in St. Petersburg! A Buddhist temple in Mallomar! What're you trying to do?

SAMUEL

You gotta touch all the bases!
(Pointing to his chest)
Don't you remember what I got in here?!

AGNES

I know, I know. A big . . . heart. *Such a big heart.*

SAMUEL

I got a triple bypass in here! That's what I got.

AGNES

At least you still got a heart. You tore mine out five years ago.

SAMUEL

Agnes, please already! You promised not to talk about that no more. The doctor said at my age and in my condition who knows how much longer I got. So tomorrow, I'm working a twelve-hour shift at the soup kitchen in —

AGNES

Oh, so now I get why all of a sudden you're Mr. Mitzvah Maker. You're trying to buy your way into heaven . . . You got a lot to atone for.

SAMUEL

Don't be ridiculous! It's because I feel for *all mankind!*

(The phone rings and AGNES answers it as SAMUEL continues talking.)

AGNES

It's your brother. He wants to talk to you.

SAMUEL

Tell that bum never to call here again!

(SAMUEL hangs up the phone.)

FANUEL

(Sticking his head out from the bedroom door)

Not good enough. Definitely not good enough for upstairs!

AGNES

You won't talk to your own brother but you have this shlemiel sleeping in our home! In the room our daughter should be in. This I cannot stand! Tell him to get out of here and go back the hell to his park bench.

SAMUEL

But, Agnes, it's cold out there.

AGNES

Then send him to those people upstairs he's always talking about.

SAMUEL

What upstairs? I think maybe he's not right in the head.

AGNES

One meshugene in the house is all I can stand, Samuel. I've been a good wife to you, but since your bypass —

SAMUEL

Triple bypass!

AGNES

Since that day, I don't understand you anymore. It's me or him, Samuel — either he goes or I go!

SAMUEL

But, but . . . I already wrote his name in my book.

AGNES

(To FANUEL)

All of a sudden you're so quiet. Well, what do you have to say for yourself about this?

FANUEL

Can I have another bagel before I go to sleep?

AGNES

That's it! I'm leaving! Call me when he's gone. Then maybe I'll come back.

SAMUEL

Agnes, have a heart!

AGNES

I told you — I don't have one anymore!

(She walks out of the apartment.)

SAMUEL

Agnes . . . come back! You didn't eat your bagel!
(To FANUEL)
She's gone. And . . . and . . .
(Pointing his finger at FANUEL)
And it's all your fault!

FANUEL

But I thought it was your brother Jake's fault.

SAMUEL

How do you know my brother's name? Huh?

FANUEL

(Ignoring his question)
That's why you wouldn't talk to him on the phone, isn't it?

SAMUEL

You don't know what you're talking —

FANUEL

I mean it couldn't possibly be your fault what happened . . . could it? Your fault that your daughter's bedroom is —

SAMUEL

Listen you . . . you park bench pisher . . . you don't know how to keep your nose out of other people's business. Just like my brother Jake.

FANUEL

So you tell me! What terrible thing did Jake do to you?

SAMUEL

He gave my daughter money to go to college, that bastard!

FANUEL

(Looking upward)
You see what he complains about? He's not an easy case.

SAMUEL

You'd better stop talking to yourself before they send you somewhere. And it ain't gonna' be the park!

FANUEL

(Still looking upward)
See? See what I mean?

SAMUEL

Okay! If you wanna talk to the ceiling, why don't you tell them this — I had a business, a family business, making cardboard boxes. My father started it here in New York after he escaped Germany in the '30s when those brown-shirt bastards were ruining our lives. You know about that?

FANUEL

Know about it? I was there!

SAMUEL

There!? How could you —

FANUEL

And the family business?

SAMUEL

My father took me into the business when I was sixteen . . . didn't finish school . . . who needed it? Worked there until five years ago.

FANUEL

That sounds like an awful lot of boxes, Samuel.

SAMUEL

Damn right! I had cardboard up my kazoo for over fifty years.

FANUEL

And what else did you have, Samuel?

SAMUEL

Whaddaya mean?

FANUEL

You know what I mean.

SAMUEL

Yeah, well, I had a lot of things.

FANUEL

But what was the most important thing to you?

SAMUEL

Ah, what do you know about me? You're just some homeless shlemiel from the —

FANUEL

What was it, Samuel? The most important thing? What was it?

SAMUEL

All right, all right! My daughter, my daughter. When you only got one kid . . . they become so important to . . . then they let you down. That goddamn triple bypass!

FANUEL

And the family business?

SAMUEL

What family business? Gone. Seventy years in the family . . . gone! No son . . . just a daughter who thought she was too good to run a cardboard box company. That bastard, brother of mine!

FANUEL

You hate him because he gave her money to go to college when she wouldn't take over the company. That's not good, Samuel. Not good at all.

SAMUEL

See, you do agree with me!

FANUEL

I didn't mean your brother was no good, I meant —

SAMUEL

A designer! A designer she had to be . . . like the world doesn't have enough! Ah, but what's the use of talking . . . I don't have a daughter any more. She hasn't set foot in this house since —

(A knock on the door. SAMUEL stares at the door in silence. Another knock. SAMUEL freezes in place.)

FANUEL

Let me help you.

(He opens the door and lets in SARAH.)

SARAH

Hello, Father. Don't worry, I only came because of Mother. How is she?

SAMUEL

Sarah, Sarah . . . you are here?

SARAH

Please, Father, is Mother all right?

SAMUEL

Uh, uh, Mother. Yes, yes, she is — what made you think there was a problem with —

SARAH

I got a phone call from a man who said there was an emergency —

FANUEL

(Looking upward)

A little white lie! You said I was allowed two a month.

SAMUEL

No, no your mother is fine, there must have been a —

SARAH

Then there is no reason for me to be —

(She turns to leave apartment.)

SAMUEL

No, don't —

SARAH

No, don't what? Go to college? It's too late for that. Five years too late. I have my degree now.

SAMUEL

Have you no shame? Two minutes in our apartment and you are already talking about your college degree when you know what happened to the family business.

SARAH

And have you no shame talking about the business the first time I set foot in this apartment in —

SAMUEL

Ah, if that is how you still feel, I have no time for this. I have to go work in the soup kitchen . . . even a broken heart cannot stop me from —

SARAH

Your broken heart? No more broken than mine, Father.

FANUEL

They say if you take two broken hearts and put them together, you get a whole heart once again.

SARAH

Who is this? And why does his voice sound so familiar to me?

SAMUEL

A mitzvah I did. I should get double credit for taking in such a case! This is Fanuel.

SARAH

Fanuel? Isn't that the name of the Angel of Hope and Redemption in the —

FANUEL

So, Sarah, I hear you are a designer now.

SARAH

I don't think my father wants to hear about that. I think I ought to just —

SAMUEL

No, no, you are here, so tell him already . . . before he starts eating again.

SARAH

Yes, I design men's undergarments. They're sold in all the better stores.

SAMUEL

Imagine! She let the box business die so she could make underwear!

FANUEL

And cardboard boxes are so fancy-shmancy, Samuel?

SAMUEL

(Pondering)

Well, maybe you got a point —

FANUEL

And she makes such gorgeous briefs too!

SARAH

(Moving closer to him)

You know my brand of undergarments?

FANUEL

Know it? What a fit! Here, let me show you.

(Starting to open his bathrobe)

SAMUEL

Hey! Hey! Stop! That's my daughter there.

SARAH

Look, Father, this is getting crazy. I'd better go.

(Walking to the door)

Please tell Mother I was —

SAMUEL

Wait, wait! Maybe you got some underwear for me, too? Your mother's always trying to get me to throw out all my old torn shorts. How about it?

FANUEL

Ha, that's good, Samuel. Very good!

SARAH

You'd actually wear my underwear? You told me once you'd set fire to them if —

SAMUEL

I wear size forty-two. You got 'em?

SARAH

I do, but not with me. I could ship you out a half dozen —

SAMUEL

You do that, my mailman'll end up wearing 'em to his son's bar mitzvah. Why don't you bring 'em over here yourself?

SARAH

You mean it? You'd really like me to come back here?

SAMUEL

Yeah, yeah, how about today? We can have lunch!

FANUEL

Mazel tov! I'll go out and get more everything bagels and lox!

SAMUEL

I'll tell your Mother you're coming. She'll be so happy to see you, Sarah . . . What do you think, huh?

SARAH

I've waited so long for you to —

SAMUEL

Your father has been a very stupid man. Can you find it in your heart to forgive him?

SARAH

Oh, Dad!

(SARAH runs over to hug her father who gives her a long hug in return. Then she goes to front door.)

I'll be back by noon . . . with the underwear!

SAMUEL

And Sarah . . . maybe after, we could work in the soup kitchen together. Huh? Maybe get your Uncle Jake, my crazy brother, to come along.

SARAH

(Heading for the door)
Sure, Dad, sure! Sounds great!

(She exits.)

FANUEL

(Looking upward)

He's good enough now! I think he's in. What about you?

(To SAMUEL)

That was inspiring, Samuel. You don't have to worry about making any more mitzvahs.

SAMUEL

I got my daughter back. That's what really counts! But a few more hours in the soup kitchen . . .

(Looking upwards)

That couldn't hurt, right? And, and . . . hey, what size underwear you guys wear? I'm gonna bring some with me when I get up there! Just not too soon . . . if it's okay with you.

(Slow fadeout)

The End

The Empty Seder Chair

Milton Polsky

Photo by Andrew Benjamin

Samuel and Leah welcome their son, Isaac, home from the Civil War.

CHARACTERS

Corporal Jeremy Johnson, Black Union soldier, his arm in a sling, about 20
Samuel Ackerman, Union uniform supplier, about 65
Leah, his wife, about 60
Major Isaac Ackerman, their son, a Union Army cartographer, his hand in a cast, about 25

TIME

Monday, April 10, 1865, early evening

PLACE

The dining room of Samuel Ackerman, in Washington, D.C. A table festively set for Passover with five chairs. There is a window, off to the side.

(MUSIC: Short pre-opening bridge. A rousing historic U.S. military march, blending into traditional Hebraic tunes, then out. JEREMY, arm in sling, hands ISAAC a small, nicely wrapped package.)

ISAAC

How is that arm, Jeremy?

JEREMY

Barely well enough to hand you that, Sir.

ISAAC

No need for "sirring" me, Jeremy. War's over. Hurrah!

(He puts package on table.)

JEREMY

Yes, hurrah, praise God . . . Here's my mother's special dessert treat for your seder, Isaac. She thanks you all for your kindness.

ISAAC

Maybe . . . you could join us . . .

JEREMY

Me?
(Laughing gently)
I hardly think so—

(SAMUEL enters with a tray of wine glasses.)

SAMUEL

Ah, good day, Jeremy . . .

JEREMY

And to you, Mr. Ackerman, sir. I'm on my way to church with a full heart of joy, praise God—

SAMUEL

A great day for Heaven's blessings. Your mother is with your aunt in Baltimore?

JEREMY

Yes, a mite too far for me to travel to Baltimore to see my cousins. Have a good seder. All the best to Mrs. Ackerman and to you, Isaac.

(He and ISAAC hug, a bit awkwardly, and JEREMY exits with a little bow to SAMUEL.)

SAMUEL

Isaac, I've been thinking . . .

(He and ISAAC look over table set with some traditional Passover symbols.)

ISAAC

No, Pa, don't start . . . I just got back . . . I need to breathe . . .

SAMUEL

Of course, but —

ISAAC

No more for me. The whole country's like one big fortress covered with dead bodies. I've seen enough of it! I'll stay put right here.

SAMUEL

This time is different, Isaac. So many broken, smoldering cities, and towns — so, so much new building to do 'cross the land. And engineers are needed — really needed —to help the healing . . .

ISAAC

Healing? That's not the feeling I get. So much damned resentment, hatred, from the mouths of those defeated rebels.

SAMUEL

(Picking up Haggadah from table)

But it says right in here, in the Haggadah, we went out from Egypt as one people . . . I do believe from this war we will come out one country, like our president said, to bind the wounds of this nation.

ISAAC

Well, not so quick. The nation will have its own scorching desert to face.

SAMUEL

Maybe so, but still, West Point has the only Engineering School in America. Listen, son, you served in the Engineering Corp with honor and were picked on the field of duty to be an officer. Now you can be certified as an engineer at West Point to qualify for a civilian position — a good life.

ISAAC
I'd prefer helping you remodel the store and, we can vary your merchandise more in the factory, too, and —

SAMUEL
You want to spend the rest of your life in a pants and shirts store and its factory, do you? Throwing away a chance for a career of civic service because you —

ISAAC
Finish it — because I — because I want to help your black workers with their jobs!

SAMUEL
That's not the part I object to. They already know how to make pants —

ISAAC
Well, on that I well-nigh agree . . . so why shouldn't they get the same payment for the same work as your white workers?

SAMUEL
So there, admit it! Why you really want to stay here is to alter my payscale. I won't put up with you interfering with my business —

ISAAC
Just to make it equitable — just as the black soldiers are now getting the same pay as white soldiers.
(Walking around the table)
Where does this horseradish go?

(SAMUEL points where. LEAH comes in carrying a tray full of matzos.)

LEAH
You two arguing again? Sam, please. He just got back —

(LEAH puts plate of matzos on table.)

ISAAC
Jeremy just brought this over, Ma. His mother made some dessert from her kitchen.

LEAH
Ah, how thoughtful of her. Well, she's waited a long time for this day of liberation for her people in the South . . .

(ISAAC exits.)

I hope our special guest enjoys his dish. I hear he usually favors milk, fruit, with his bread for dinner — so the matzo may be a —
(Pauses, smilingly finds the right word)
A revelation of sorts . . .

(They both have a good laugh. LEAH exits with the package as ISAAC returns.)

SAMUEL

Isaac, now that the bloody war is over, I propose a toast —
(Picks up a wine bottle and pours a glass)

LEAH

(Returning)
Wait — wait —

SAMUEL

Okay, all right —

LEAH

You give it, son —

(SAMUEL nods.)

ISAAC

Well . . . To everlasting peace and harmony in a united country — only yesterday — a day marked in history, April 9, when General Robert E. Lee surrendered to our good General U. S. Grant — uniting our country . . .

SAMUEL

Yes, to one country—

(Puts on cap and says Hebrew blessing before the wine. They all say Amen.)

ISAAC

(Sipping)
Azoy gut, Pa. And the wine's pasteurized, I assume?

SAMUEL

That's right — it started this year. A toast to Louis Pasteur, for the best in wine and milk. Good health! And peace at long last!

ISAAC

(Pointing)

Those two chairs besides us — for Aunt Rebecca and Uncle Phillip?

SAMUEL

No, they can't make it tonight.

ISAAC

Who else—?

LEAH

Oh, someone very special . . . and his wife, special, too.

SAMUEL

Sshh—

LEAH

Shush yourself. You're a dreamer, Sam. Why would he come here?

ISAAC

I know! Elijah, the prophet who rose to heaven in a fiery chariot and manages to visit every Jewish family in the world at the same time—

LEAH

Faster than the telegraph wire with the news of Lee's surrender.

ISAAC

I should've been with my regiment cheering them on instead of on furlough with my useless broken hand —

SAMUEL

Please, Izzy — your only furlough in four years of fighting—

ISAAC

So who could it be? Maybe our nervous Mr. Secretary of War Stanton himself?

(A pause, a weary smile)

No, don't tell me. I've had enough surprises in my life . . .

(Turning to LEAH)

By the way, Ma, Jeremy was so pleased you let his mother off early today.

SAMUEL

Well, only fitting, Grace wanting to celebrate the end of the war with her relatives and friends in Baltimore. Yes, the barbeque, the fireworks and all. You

SAMUEL (Cont'd)

know, I plan to hire Jeremy in the factory—

ISAAC

Good, Pa — I hope at the same wage as —

SAMUEL

We'll discuss that after Passover—

(Silence)

LEAH

(Attempting to break the tension in the air)

After the holiday, maybe we can all go theater next week —

ISAAC

Oh, not in that silly farce, *Our American Cousin.*

LEAH

(Teasingly)

Oh, Would you prefer a nice French very light opera perhaps?

ISAAC

(An embarrassed chuckle)

No, thanks, I think I'm a bit too old for that, but when I was stationed in New York I saw a production of *Julius Caesar* at the Winter Garden starring the three Booth brothers — Junius Jr., Edwin, and John Wilkes, too — well, Southerners, but superb actors —

LEAH

(Laughing)

Did you know, son, I once dreamed of becoming an actress? Silly of me . . .

ISAAC

(Lightly)

No, Ma — but then you could've been really special on stage —

LEAH

(A brief good-natured smile)

Well, I guess I'm past that stage — after years of changing diapers and then changing our soldiers' bandages . . .

ISAAC

You certainly played your part . . . and that was pretty damn tough!

ISAAC (Cont'd)

(A hasty apologetic gesture)
Sorry, should I bring in the appetizers now?

(LEAH nods. ISAAC exits.)

SAMUEL

(Looking through the window)
Where is his special guard? Should be outside surrounding every nook and cranny by now . . .

ISAAC

(Returning with a tray, smiling)
Hmm, spying around, eh? Someone really important coming?

LEAH

Tell him already, Sam, you stubborn —

SAMUEL

Very well, since you haven't guessed, I'll tell you — that big empty chair is for President Lincoln.

ISAAC

Lincoln himself? What — How'd that happen?

LEAH

Yesterday . . .

SAMUEL

I was in the store taking inventory. A carriage rolls up, and he came in with Mrs. Lincoln. She made him measure for a new pair of pants — what he was wearing had more creases than his wrinkled face — so I did and I suggested a new frock coat too . . . Well, wearing that, he looked so handsome, his wife said, She wanted to take him to the theater . . .

LEAH

Oh, I hear he loves plays — especially comedies —

ISAAC

Yes, if they're good ones.

LEAH

To make a long story short, Sam got to talking about our plans for a seder, and he said he's never been to one, so . . .

SAMUEL

Wait, let me tell him — so he was wondering if he might stop here, oh, for a short visit, mind you — uh, not to upset anything—

(Chuckles)

That was his little joke . . .

ISAAC

I think maybe he was joking, Pa, about coming.

LEAH

Hard to believe he would come with so much to do . . .

ISAAC

So while I was gone, you got to know him?

SAMUEL

Well . . . I headed up a war bonds committee . . . and, of course, I made uniforms for several regiments of the Union Army. And he's always liked my tailoring for his cabinet members.

ISAAC

You really invited him? The president? Here? Oh, God —

(Looking through window)

But it's dark, it's getting late . . . I dunno, Pa, are you sure he's coming?

SAMUEL

Patience, patience son. How long did we Jews have to wait to be liberated?

ISAAC

And the Negroes — ?

LEAH

Both of you, stop. If, God forbid, he doesn't come, so maybe he'll honor us some other time, like Hanukkah, also celebrating freedom—

(Silence)

ISAAC

Then couldn't we invite Grace's son, Jeremy? He's at church, down the block.

LEAH

Jeremy?

ISAAC

Yes, why not? When I fell off my horse at Bull Run . . . bad fall . . . he kneeled down and hoisted me up. God, what a risk he took for me!

(Silence)

SAMUEL

Wait — we'll wait. The president often takes strolls by himself. Lot of crowds tonight, with the war over. That's what delaying him . . . maybe he's walking with Secretary Seward, who will be most welcome.

ISAAC

But so should Jeremy. Pa, please — I'm talking about a man who saved me, a hero in my eyes. So many of our black troops were — are . . .

SAMUEL

(Turning to ISAAC)

I know, they say 18,000 colored men served. Brave men. Look, son, no one's denying any soldier's bravery. Yes, brave. All of you. There's something I want to show our great guest tonight—

(He exits offstage.)

LEAH

(Calling off gently)

Sam, please, maybe he's not coming, please, forget it! Let's enjoy our seder.

(SAMUEL returns, holding a large scrapbook.)

SAMUEL

I'm not ready to forget it.

(Opening the book to a page)

Wait until our president sees this! And to think you drew these while riding on a horse — amazing — on a horse!

ISAAC

(Wearily)

So who cares how I did it! It's just a patch of blood to me!

SAMUEL

(Ignoring that)

And with a word put in by Mr. Lincoln, they will be very impressed at West Point — how you served with General George Custer at Sayerville sketching locations for another Custer charge — it's yours, yes?

(He hands ISAAC the sketch.)

ISAAC

I made that sketch, yes, God help me. Please let it go, that butcher's field of dead bodies . . . please!

(He sits. LEAH stands by him as he turns away from SAMUEL. SAMUEL picks up a Haggadah.)

SAMUEL

God did decide! It was a war, like God did smite the Egyptians pursuing the Hebrew slaves . . . And this war, also God had to choose — had to choose —

ISAAC

(Quietly)
So many died, so many freed . . .

(He puts his bandaged hand to mouth, then to his eyes.)

Excuse me . . . I need air—

(He lets the sketch fall to the floor and starts to exit.)

SAMUEL

Izzy —

ISAAC

Sorry. Tears unbecoming an officer . . .

SAMUEL

(Warmly)
Come back here! No more of that — we're making this a happy time . . .
(Lightly)
Even if he doesn't come . . .

ISAAC

So couldn't we invite Jeremy?
(Rising)
I think that . . .

SAMUEL

Jeremy?
(Mulling this over)

LEAH

Grace will be overjoyed we did this for her son.

SAMUEL

(Teasingly)

Well, all right . . . but at the table tonight don't bring up anything about equal pay . . . time for that later . . .

(ISAAC nods compliantly, letting that go for now, sharing a short conciliatory smile with his father. Doorbell rings.)

(Euphoric)

Ah, so he's here—at last! You see? The good Lord has not forgotten us!

LEAH

(Hopefully starting toward the door)

Maybe not . . .

(She goes off.)

ISAAC

(Standing smartly at attention)

How do I look?

SAMUEL

Like my son . . . our son! Don't worry, he'll be proud of you as we are.

(LEAH returns.)

LEAH

The president will not be coming tonight. His messenger says God willing he will stop by next week . . . and oh, Samuel, he also conveys to you, that on Friday he will be wearing to the theater the suit you tailored for him.

SAMUEL

(Softly, with a longing glance at the empty seder chair)

So we will see him next week . . .

LEAH

Yes . . . our great luck — maybe on the last day of Passover.

SAMUEL

God's time to heal . . .

(Warmly taking ISAAC's good hand)
So for now, you can invite your friend to join us.

(ISAAC nods happily, starts off. SAMUEL and LEAH share a fond contented look, start towards the seder table. As the lights fade, and the corners darken, the last image is of the empty seder chair. MUSIC: Short closing bridge, festive Passover tunes, blending into softer recap of historic military march, then slowing, darkening into a few sad final notes.)

The End

Chekhov, Shmekhov

By Allan Yashin

Photo by Andrew Benjamin

The Russian songbird, Vera Similitude, performs for the first time in America.

CHARACTERS

Professor Gruber, theatrical impresario, about 60
Heshel Fitzinger, Gruber's boyhood friend and Broadway producer
Vera Similitude, singing sensation, 30s

TIME AND PLACE

Scene One, Today, in Gruber's studio
Scene Two, Later that day, in Heshel Fitzinger's apartment

SCENE ONE

GRUBER

(Looking intently at a script and mumbling to himself)
Anton Chekhov, a playwright of such compassion for the human condition! We are adrift in the cosmic void . . . yet hoping for a connection with a kindred spirit to help us endure the unendurable.
(Raising his hands to the heavens)
Anton, only one man has the sensitivity to give full justice to your genius . . . your devoted interpreter, Professor Phillip Gruber. I humbly await your inspiration!

HESHEL

(Walking into the room)
Who the hell are you talking to, Phil?

GRUBER

Ah, Heshel, my friend, my colleague, my dedicated patron of the arts . . . Gruber is honored by your presence at his announcement of—

HESHEL

Well, if you're so damned honored by my presence, why the hell don't you at least get my name right? It's not Heshel anymore . . . it's Harrison!

GRUBER

Heshel was plenty good for you when we were playing stickball together growing up in Brooklyn. Heshel Fitzinger . . . a nice name . . . lots of character.

HESHEL

That's a long time before I became a producer of Broadway shows. Heshel Fitzinger sounds . . . too ethnic now.

GRUBER

In New York City you're worried about sounding too ethnic?

HESHEL

It's not the people from New York I'm worried about, it's the tourists. I don't want them to get the wrong idea about my shows. That's why I changed my name to Harrison, Harrison Fitz, it's nothing too foreign-sounding.

GRUBER

Oh, now I understand. Then we better change Anton Chekhov's name to Andy Checkers. And what about that William Shakespeare guy? How about Billy Bob

Milkshake. Sound American enough?

HESHEL

Look, Phil, I didn't come here to have an argument about my name . . . I came out of an act of friendship . . . to do an old friend a favor, and hear the announcement of your —

GRUBER

A favor? A favor to me? I thought you came as a favor to the theater-goers of the world, to get the opportunity to present them with this year's holiday production of another one of the immortal works of the maestro: Anton Chekov!

HESHEL

Well, to tell you the truth, last year's production of *The Cherry Orchid* was a total disaster at the box office and —

GRUBER

Wait, my ears must be deceiving me! Did I hear you imply that you measure the merit of a production by the number of shekels dropped in your pocket?

HESHEL

Look, Gruber, that's easy for you to say! You don't have my expenses with the —

GRUBER

You can't put a price-tag on innovation! Don't you realize that you went down in theatrical history as the producer of the *The Fortune Cookie Orchid* — the first Kabuki version of a Chekhov play.

HESHEL

We made history all right — for the highest number of protestors outside a theater complaining about Asian stereotypes!

GRUBER

An artist doesn't have time for small-minded people.

HESHEL

And what about the fact that half the cast got food poisoning from that week-old sushi they ate in the last act?

GRUBER

I should know that you can't count on a pushcart on Delancey Street to sell fresh sushi? Besides, you couldn't complain about my production of Chekhov's "Seagull" . . . not an empty seat for our opening.

HESHEL

Yes, wonderful . . . except for the fact that you didn't tell me you were going to let actual seagulls fly over the audience.

GRUBER

I know! What a masterstroke of theatrical realism. I only wish Stanislavski himself had been there to see it.

HESHEL

Me too, then he could've paid the dry-cleaning bill for all the people who got shit on by those birds that night!

GRUBER

Remember what Chekhov said: "Let us learn to appreciate that there will be times when the trees are bare and look forward to the time when we will pick the fruit." If you could only emulate the artistic spirit of that saintly man instead of constantly looking at the amount in your checking account. Hmm, which reminds me, do you happen to have that $500 I asked you to loan me to pay this month's rent?

HESHEL

My wallet is bare, just like the trees.

GRUBER

Oh, you always did have such a lovely sense of humor!

(GRUBER holds out his open hand to HESHEL, who reluctantly hands him the money.)

HESHEL

You know, you can take advantage of our boyhood together in Brooklyn for just so long. You're going to bankrupt me with this Chekhov obsession of yours.

GRUBER

But my dearest friend, your financial well-being is always uppermost in my mind, that is why I have devised my latest play to have unlimited commercial potential . . . Chekhov's *Uncle Vanya . . . the Musical!* Music and lyrics by me, your humble impresario.

HESHEL

For crying out —

GRUBER

It can't miss, and do you know why?

HESHEL

Yes, I know . . . you're an innovative genius, just like with every other play you've ever —

GRUBER

So true, but also because Gruber has made the casting coup of the century. I have flown here, directly from Moscow, the legendary Soviet Songbird, Vera Similitude, to star in my production.

HESHEL

Who?

GRUBER

And here she is, for the first time ever on an American stage, to sing my "Love Song" from *Uncle Vanya!*

(GRUBER points to the wings and out walks an attractive woman who takes center stage and begins to sing)

VERA

(Singing with Russian accent)
Uncle Vanya
I wanya to love me
Uncle Vanya
I wanya to care.
I want to rid you of your old ennui
And have you make mad love to me.
We'll flee the rural estate and move to Minsk
Where I'll cook you borsht and cherry blintz.
We'll lie beneath those glorious Russian stars
And I'll
let you be
my little commissar
Oh, Uncle Vanya
I wanya to —

HESHEL

Chekhov, Shmekhov! I've had it!

VERA

(Speaking with Russian accent)
Excusing me? Is you be having a problem?

HESHEL

I'm sorry, you have a lovely voice, this isn't about you. It's about Gruber and his —

GRUBER

I can't believe you stopped the fabled Similitude in the middle of a song! There may be international repercussions!

HESHEL

I don't care if the damned UN calls an emergency General Assembly meeting! I'm not sinking another dime of my money into your crackpot ideas!

(HESHEL hurries out of the room. GRUBER and VERA stare at one another.)

GRUBER

You know, he's got the same bad temper he had when we were growing up in Flatbush.

VERA

(Speaking with a New York accent)
You guys from Brooklyn were always so aggressive!

GRUBER

Yes, certainly not up to the standards of you exalted Queens girls.

VERA

You promised that if I spoke with a Russian accent I could count on being in your play, but your old friend just ran out of here. Now what?

GRUBER

Have no fear, my lovely, it's only a matter of time until you'll be starring on the Great White Way in *Uncle Vanya . . . the Musical!*

VERA

And what makes you so sure of that?

GRUBER

Because Heshel has one weak spot I know we can exploit. Here's my plan . . .

End of Scene

(Lights fade down and up.)

SCENE TWO

HESHEL

(Looking at script)
Uncle Vanya . . . the Musical! That Gruber is delusional if he thinks —
(A knock on his apartment door)
That's probably him on his hands and knees. Well, it won't work this time!

(HESHEL opens the door, finding VERA standing there.)

Vera Similitude! What're you doing here?

VERA

(Speaking with Russian accent)
I could not keep myself away! I saw the way you look at me when I was singing.

HESHEL

Well, yes, you certainly are very attractive, can't deny that, but —

VERA

And I felt your doo-shah — what we Russians call our soul — calling out to me . . .

HESHEL

My grandfather did come to America from Saint Petersburg, but —

VERA

I feel as if we had met somewhere before, perhaps in another life.

HESHEL

Yes, I think I saw that movie.

VERA

And this time I do not want to let you slip away.

(She tries to touch his face.)

HESHEL

(Moving her hand away)
Look, Vera, if all of this is about your trying to convince me to put on Gruber's play . . . well, it's a waste of time. He sent you here, didn't he?

VERA

But this Gruber is a genius, no?

HESHEL

A genius at emptying out my bank account. If I'm going to lose money, I might as well do it on my own.

VERA

So . . . *Uncle Vanya . . . the Musical!* is, as you say, kaput?

HESHEL

Absolutely! I've devoted enough of my life on his artistic vision. Now, I'm finally going to do something for myself.

VERA

Then yes, you must do something of your own passion — something from your doo-shah.

HESHEL

You're right, I will . . . I mean I have . . . here, here . . . wait, I want to show you something I've never shown to anyone before. It's a play I've written. And I think someone from Russia like you might really understand it.

(HESHEL takes a script off his desk and hands it to VERA.)

It's the story of my grandfather's life when he first came to America. How he had to do menial labor because he only spoke Russian, but then he went to a class for immigrants to teach them English and he fell in love with the teacher of the class who was this beautiful young woman from Queens.

VERA

And did that teacher lady love him, too?

HESHEL

The amazing part is that yes, yes she did! They got married. She was my grandmother.

VERA

A love story . . . so wonderful.

HESHEL

And to tell you the truth, you actually look just like pictures of my grandmother when she was your age. You know, you'd be perfect in the role.

VERA

You be meaning that?

HESHEL

When I saw you this morning, I immediately thought about you for the part. You're so lovely, the whole audience could see why my grandfather loved you. What a shame, though.

VERA

A shame? What is this shame?

HESHEL

My grandmother came from Queens and spoke perfect English. If only you didn't have that Russian accent.

VERA

Da! Such a shame! But . . . I saw many American movies when I lived in Moscow. Maybe I could do good American accent. I try . . .
(Speaking in her natural voice)
So, what do you think, Heshel? Do I sound like a girl who grew up in Queens to you?

HESHEL

It's perfect! You've got the part!

VERA

Oh, thank you so much!

(She gives him a "thank you" kiss which then turns into a more romantic kiss between them.)

HESHEL

(Holding VERA in his arms)
Kissing my own grandmother! How do you say "kinky" in Russian?

VERA

(Stepping away from HESHEL)
I can't go on with this anymore. I've been lying to you. I really am from Queens after all.

HESHEL

(In mock amazement)
No! I can't believe it!

VERA

What?

HESHEL

Vera, I knew you weren't really Russian from the first minute you opened your mouth to sing this morning! Gruber doesn't have enough money to pay an actresses bus fare from Jersey, let alone import one from Moscow.

VERA

Well, I am just so sorry for trying to fool you.

HESHEL

Don't be. The theater is all about illusion, isn't it? It was just Gruber's way of trying to make his production seem more authentic. I know how his distorted mind works after all these years.

VERA

So you're not angry with me? I can still play your grandmother?

HESHEL

(Taking VERA into his arms again)

Well, it may take a little personal coaching in my family history from the playwright.

VERA

Hmm . . . I'd love that!

(A loud knock on the door. GRUBER bursts in and sees them embracing.)

GRUBER

Ahh! Love in flower! As Chekhov says, "It is our sole refuge from the constant onslaught of the inevitable!" So, when does my *Uncle Vanya . . . the Musical!* go into production?

HESHEL

I'm sorry, my old friend, it's not going to happen.

GRUBER

What! But I rented Yankee Stadium . . . on your credit card, of course . . .

HESHEL

I'm going to be producing a show starring Vera.

VERA

Can you believe it? I'm going to play his grandmother.

GRUBER

(Sarcastically)

Surprise, surprise! And such a good American accent too! It will be lovely, no doubt. But *Uncle Vanya* is a classic that has endured the —

VERA

And I fall in love with his grandfather!

HESHEL

Yes, after he comes here from Russia in 1910 to work on the docks of New York.

GRUBER

Hmm! The story of an immigrant coming to a new land . . .

HESHEL

And they leave New York and travel by freight train to the wheat fields of Minnesota, where they raise a family of ten children who —

GRUBER

It's an American saga! I can see it now . . . for the first act the audience sits on blankets in Battery Park, the stage lit by the lights of the Statue of Liberty as your grandfather crawls soaking wet out of the harbor —

HESHEL

It didn't actually happen that way, but —

GRUBER

Then at intermission we'll have a hundred boats in the Hudson River and we'll have the audience row to the Jersey Meadowlands where we'll have built a wooden farmhouse and planted a hundred acres of wheat!

HESHEL

It sounds crazy but it just might —

GRUBER

The audience will be given sickles and bushels and they'll harvest the wheat while Vera sings to your grandfather.

VERA

Yes, Gruber, yes! What will I sing?

GRUBER

You came thousands of miles from Russia
To harvest this wheat.
Did you ever imagine
it would be this neat
to help provide bread
eaten across our United States?
But I've got to get back to the farmhouse
I can feel the contractions
Here comes
kid number eight.

What do you think, Heshel?

HESHEL

Gruber, you're a madman . . . but the world has never seen anything like this before. I'll do it! And Vera . . . this will make you the biggest star on Broadway . . . or at least the Jersey swamplands.

(HESHEL and VERA embrace.)

GRUBER

Chekhov, Shmekhov! This . . . .will truly be my masterpiece!

(GRUBER hurries towards the front door.)

HESHEL

Gruber, where the hell are you going?

GRUBER

To Delancey Street . . . I've got to buy a hundred rowboats for the show!

(Blackout)

The End

The Polish Girl

Allan Yashin

Photo by Andrew Benjamin

Martin and his long-lost niece share a secret.

CHARACTERS

Martin, 50s
Sandra, his wife, 50s
Paulina, 20s

TIME

A summer afternoon in 1965

PLACE

A modest apartment in New York City

MARTIN

(Looking in a mirror and straightening his tie)

How do I look?

SANDRA

Like an old man.

MARTIN

Oh, that's nice!

SANDRA

(Adjusting his tie)

But a distinguished old man. A handsome, distinguished-looking old man.

MARTIN

Well, I'm nervous enough already without your little jokes.

SANDRA

Now, dearest, there's nothing to worry about. I'm sure everything will work out perfectly.

MARTIN

How can you be so sure?

SANDRA

The sound of her voice when she called. She sounded so . . . well, so sincerely happy to hear from us . . . to know she had family in the United States.

MARTIN

I owe it all to your brilliant idea to put ads in those newspapers in Poland.

SANDRA

I know how much finding her meant to you.

MARTIN

She's my niece . . . my brother's little girl. What else could I do?

SANDRA

If only he'd listened to you in 1938, and come to America like you did.

MARTIN

He always was a stubborn ox. "You're going to let those Nazi fools chase you from your own country? Be a man and stand your ground!" Yeah, like those brown-shirted bastards cared about his ground. Ah, I should've made him listen to me!

SANDRA

You've got to stop blaming yourself. At least he had the sense to send his daughter off to a family that was willing to hide a young Jewish girl before he ran off and hid in the woods.

MARTIN

Never knowing what happened to her after the war, that's what killed him. That Polish family that took her in when she was four, they were gone. You know . . . you know what he made me promise.

SANDRA

And you have, darling. For nearly twenty years you've eaten yourself up alive, trying to keep that promise to your brother. And now you've finally found her.

MARTIN

(Hugging her)
God has been very slow to answer my prayers. I'm sorry I made things so hard for us all these years.

SANDRA

That's all right. The waiting's finally over.

(A knock on the door)
That must be her now!

MARTIN

(Opening the door)
Paulina? Is it really you?

PAULINA

(Carrying luggage)
Yes, it is me, Uncle Martin!

(PAULINA puts down her luggage and throws her arms around MARTIN's neck.)

MARTIN

(Holding her at arm's length with hands on both her shoulders)
To see you here at last, it's like a miracle! You're just the way I pictured you.

PAULINA

(Speaking with Polish accent)

To me the miracle was reading the newspaper in Warsaw and seeing that an American family was searching for years and years for their missing niece. Paulina Landowski, daughter of Jakub and Josefa.

SANDRA

But you told me your last name is Kraska.

PAULINA

Yes . . . it is the name of the family that adopted me. But I always remember the name of my real mama and poppa. And the newspaper said I had last been living in Olsztyn. Yes, that is where we lived until the Kraskas moved to Warsaw.

MARTIN

Ah, they probably moved to a big city so it would be that much harder to find you after the war was over. The bastards!

PAULINA

No, no bastards. They loved me. Did not want to give me up if my family come looking for me.

MARTIN

Well, I can only tell you how much your father's heart was broken when he could not find you after the war.

SANDRA

And I can't tell you how happy your Uncle Martin has been since you contacted us. Now I'm going to leave you two alone. I know there must be so much you want to say to each other.

(She kisses MARTIN on the cheek.)

(To PAULINA)

Welcome to the family.

(She kisses PAULINA on the cheek and leaves the room.)

PAULINA

You are lucky to have such wonderful wife. Not every lady be happy to have new strange person in her family.

MARTIN

Yes, I am lucky, but you are no strange person, you are our niece. My brother's only child. It's so amazing . . . after all these years, you are here in New York. Tell me, have you ever been to America before?

PAULINA

Only in my dreams.

MARTIN

So tell me about your life in Poland.

PAULINA

Life in Poland?

MARTIN

Yes, yes. Where do you live ?

PAULINA

Yes, still live in Warsaw.

MARTIN

By yourself? Or still with the Kraskas?

PAULINE

With Kraskas? No, no more. I have my own flat in Warsaw. More easy to do that . . . not like in New York City.

MARTIN

People in Poland know that about New York?

PAULINE

Uh, yes, we see on TV. New York . . . ex-pen-sive, yes?
(Silence as MARTIN stares at PAULINA)
Much money to live in Man-hat-tan . . . yes?

MARTIN

Oh . . . yes, yes. Excuse me for staring, but you look so familiar. It must be the family resemblance.

PAULINA

Oh, yes, for me too! I look you and see my poppa.

MARTIN

Yes, who would've believed after all these years . . . But, but tell me, what do you do in Warsaw?

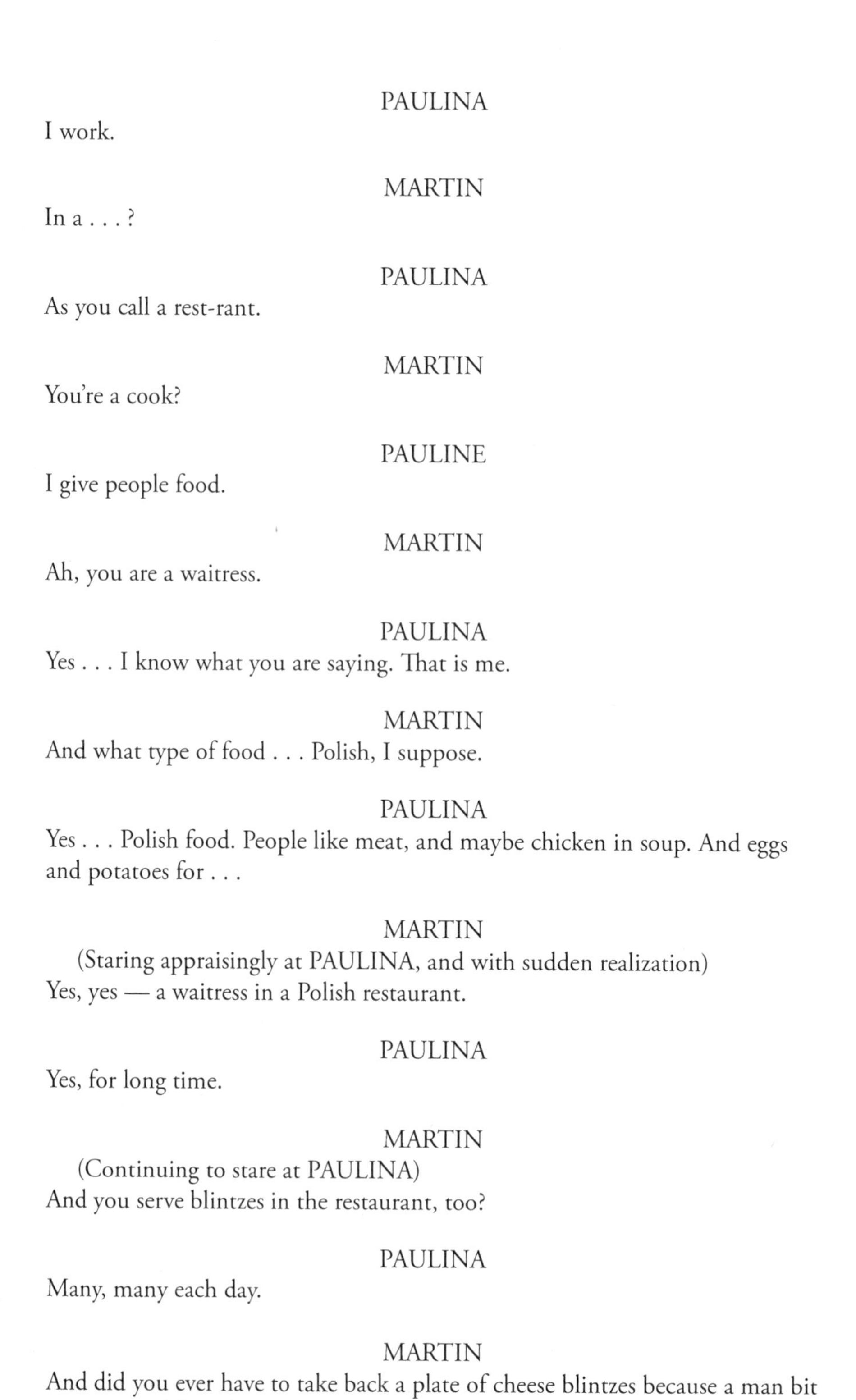

PAULINA

I work.

MARTIN

In a . . . ?

PAULINA

As you call a rest-rant.

MARTIN

You're a cook?

PAULINE

I give people food.

MARTIN

Ah, you are a waitress.

PAULINA

Yes . . . I know what you are saying. That is me.

MARTIN

And what type of food . . . Polish, I suppose.

PAULINA

Yes . . . Polish food. People like meat, and maybe chicken in soup. And eggs and potatoes for . . .

MARTIN

(Staring appraisingly at PAULINA, and with sudden realization)

Yes, yes — a waitress in a Polish restaurant.

PAULINA

Yes, for long time.

MARTIN

(Continuing to stare at PAULINA)

And you serve blintzes in the restaurant, too?

PAULINA

Many, many each day.

MARTIN

And did you ever have to take back a plate of cheese blintzes because a man bit into one and found a dollar bill inside?

PAULINA

(Gasping in shock and covering her mouth with her hands)
It is you! Oh my Gott!

MARTIN

That's right. The Warsaw Cafe . . . uptown . . . Broadway and 118 Street . . . about a year ago. I was eating brunch —

PAULINA

Yes, yes — with that red-head lady who was yelling at me.

MARTIN

(In a hushed voice)
Forget about the woman.
(In a normal voice)
Let's talk about you. You didn't really just get here from Poland, did you?

PAULINA

No, I did not.

MARTIN

And I suppose you're really not the daughter of Jakub and Josefa Landowski either, are you?

PAULINA

Customer leave Polish newspaper in restaurant. I see you are looking for girl. Think this is my chance. I am so sorry!

MARTIN

You're sorry? Why would you do this? Lie about such a thing!

PAULINA

I did bad thing, but it is because I want to stay in America. I can not get green card sponsor . . . so I must move from job to job. Work in one Polish rest-rant for few weeks then move to nother, then 'nother, then 'nother. I am here, but not really here.

MARTIN

So why don't you just go back home?

PAULINA

What home? House to house to house then orphanage where people put me, when I was ten. Throw me in street when I be eighteen.

MARTIN

Then do you know who you're birthparents really are?

PAULINA

Nobody knows no more.

MARTIN

So how did you get to America?

PAULINA

Meet handsome man, tell me he love me. Bring me to America . . . Chicago . . . then he tells me he is married and wants to take me into bed with his wife. So I run to New York — two years ago.

MARTIN

That's all so terrible . . .

PAULINA

Yes, I am terrible. I am sorry one more time. I will go now.
(Turns to leave apartment)

MARTIN

No, you are not terrible. And I don't want you to go. I want to help you.

PAULINA

Help me? Why would you do this? Do you want to take me into bed with your red-head lady?

MARTIN

Please, I beg you, don't mention her again.

PAULINA

Then why you want to help this Polish girl?

MARTIN

Because my search of almost twenty years for my niece has led to this — to you coming to my home. If this is what God wishes, then let it be so. So, please if you would let me, I will sponsor you for your green card.

PAULINA

Oh my Gott! You would do this for me? How can I ever repay you?

MARTIN

Your gift to me will be the pleasure of having a sweet young girl bring new life into our family. You could join us for the holidays. Are you Jewish?

PAULINA

I don't really know.

MARTIN

Then maybe you are.

PAULINA

Yes, maybe I am!

MARTIN

Definitely Polish, like me, and maybe a Jew — perfect!

PAULINA

Should we now tell your wife I am not your niece?

MARTIN

No, no, no, my wife was so happy that she helped me find my niece. I don't want her to be disappointed. Let her think you really are my brother's daughter. This will be our secret, you agree?

PAULINA

How can I deny you that after what you have done for me?

MARTIN

Besides, you look so much like the picture of my niece when she was three years old at her birthday party. Here, let me find it. You will be amazed!

(MARTIN leaves the room.)

SANDRA

(Entering the room, speaking in a conspiratorial tone)
So, did he believe everything I told you to tell him? That you saw the ad in a newspaper when you were working in Poland?

MARTIN

(Calling from the other room)
Sandra, did you take my nieces picture? I can't find it anywhere!

SANDRA

(Calling to MARTIN)
It's in there somewhere. Keep looking!
(To PAULINA)
It must've been God's hand that led me to read that review in the *Times* that said the Warsaw Cafe uptown had the best blintzes in New York. And there you were! The same face as his three-year-old niece. I knew this was my chance to make him a happy man. But he can't know you're not really his niece. It has to be our secret.

PAULINA

Yes, of course I can do this for you.

MARTIN

(Coming in from the other room holding a picture)
Oh, Sandra, isn't it simply wonderful to have our niece here with us. Give her a big hug to welcome her into the family.

(As SANDRA and PAULINA hug, he stands behind SANDRA and puts his finger to his lips and gives the "keep a secret sign" to PAULINA.)

SANDRA

Now it's your turn Martin. Don't be shy, you've waited twenty years for this moment.

(As MARTIN and PAULINA hug, SANDRA stands behind MARTIN and puts her finger to her lips and gives the "keep a secret sign" to PAULINA.)

(After the hug, MARTIN and SANDRA stand on either side of PAULINA, each with an arm around her shoulder.)

MARTIN

(To PAULINA as he looks at the photo in his hand)
Like a little princess at her party.

(Handing the photo to PAULINA)
Amazing, so much the same — look.

PAULINA

Oh my Gott!

MARTIN

What is it?!?

PAULINA

I remember that birthday dress! From last party before my daddy sends me away.

(In tears, she gives MARTIN a big hug.)

I am home Uncle Martin, I am home!

(Fade to black.)

The End

The Kiddush Cup

Milton Polsky

Photo by: Andrew Benjamin

Rabbi Singleton confronts the shul president.

CHARACTERS

Rabbi Jonathan Singleton, mid-70s
Danny Greenberg, his bar mitzvah student, 12
Ben Sorkin, president of the temple, about 30

TIME

A fall day, about six o'clock

PLACE

A small room, Rrabbi's office in a shul. Desk, chairs, Jewish knickknacks here and there

(MUSIC: Eclectic, light, soft in B.G.)

(RABBI SINGLETON, back to audience, straightening out his desk, finds a folder from a pile of them.)

BEN (VOICE O.S.)

(Opening door slightly. MUSIC: Out.)

Rabbi, there's a young man waiting—

RABBI SINGLETON

And where, may I ask, is our newest prodigy?

BEN (VOICE, O.S.)

With me, out here . . . I'm back from our board meeting, we have to talk . . . soon . . .

(He exits. DANNY GREENBERG, a shy twelve-year-old, enters RABBI SINGLETON's office. The RABBI is in his mid-70s, on the edge of senility, maybe a little off. Still brilliant in his confused, learned way, he can outtalk anyone. Trim beard, white shirt, loosened tie. He shakes DANNY's hand.)

RABBI SINGLETON

(Warmly)

Come in, come in. Close the door or leave it open. Have a seat.

(DANNY nods; RABBI SINGLETON sits.)

Very nice to meet with you, uh . . .

DANNY

Danny . . . Daniel Greenberg . . .

RABBI SINGLETON

Hi, Danny. Sit, please, sit.

(DANNY does. RABBI SINGLETON looks through folder.)

Grade eight, graduating in June . . . Good. In the eyes of God, June is undoubtedly good. Good high school you're going to, of course?

(DANNY nods.)

Hmm, you like theatre . . . me, too, used to perform in college. Not yet religiously, of course . . . Ah, I see you're scheduled to be a January bar mitzvah, the new year. Unsurpassably good. We'll simply finish the portion of Joseph, mid December, mid-January, Moses and his troops arrive at Mt. Sinai after devoutly departing Egypt . . . with the power of God's outstretched arm, of course —

(BEN enters, nattily dressed in suit. He's tired, on edge.)

RABBI SINGLETON

So you like plays? Hey, maybe you can direct one with the kids in our youth program —

BEN

(Sotto)

What's left of it . . .

RABBI SINGLETON

Please, Ben . . . Let me show you something, Danny, right . . . to get the wheels of your mind rollin' 'round a little.

(He takes out an ornate-looking silver goblet from his desk drawer. BEN puts his hand to his head, mutters under his breath.)

Danny, this is Mr. Sorkin, the president of our temple . . . meet Danny.

(BEN shakes DANNY's hand.)

Can you give us . . . ten minutes or so, Ben . . . I want to get Danny started on his bar mitzvah journey . . . okay? . . . I . . .

BEN

Well . . . I guess . . . Nice meeting you, Danny. I'll be next door, in my office, Rabbi . . . It's important . . .

(Starts to leave)

RABBI SINGLETON

You can leave the door open, Ben . . . So you just had a meeting on me?

(BEN sort of nods, exits. RABBI shakes his head, shrugs.)

Okay, where were we? Oh, yes. David, this is a kiddush cup . . . very, very old, take a good look, feel it . . . kiddush . . . means blessing . . . with wine, of course . . . very expensive . . . this real silver cup — the wine I don't know about.

RABBI SINGLETON (Cont'd)

(DANNY holds on to it for a few seconds.)

Look closely.Tell me, what do you see? Go ahead . . . take your time . . .

DANNY

Well . . . Some people on a bridge . . . or something . . . looking down at the water — and underneath that, a pretty design of some sort . . . running underneath the waves . . . I guess.

RABBI SINGLETON

Guessing is good, sometimes . . . yes, very pretty border around that cup. But who are these people looking down at the water? We're not sure, I'm not, anyway . . . you?

(DANNY shrugs.)

It may be they're saying good-bye . . . Danny, this cup could be from the time Jews had to leave Spain — not on their own, mind you . . . they were forced out, expelled, and maybe someone took this cup along with them on the sly, sort of . . .

DANNY

Spies or something?

RABBI SINGLETON

Hmm . . . interesting . . . Well, you see, hope springs eternal. . . . May be a blessing being forced out of Spain, expelled in 1492. Now, here's a connection. In your portion of the Torah you'll be reading and singing — with the help of God, Cantor Rabin, and yours truly — you will come to understand how the Jews in Egypt left on their own — how important the matter of choice is in life — and how not having a choice in certain things can be important too — So there will be lots for you think about. What do you say?

DANNY

Uh . . . I . . . need to go to the, uh, bathroom . . .

RABBI SINGLETON

Say no more . . . Gallop back . . . Can you close the door behind you now? Thanks.

(DANNY exits as BEN reenters and closes the door.)

So?

BEN

Listen, I heard that, what's with that meshugene kiddush cup again? Very expensive? Did you forget where this cup came from?

RABBI SINGLETON

Refresh me: Was it a long time? Before the Exodus or after the Expulsion?

BEN

Not funny!

RABBI SINGLETON

(Confused)

Funny? I wasn't trying to be.

BEN

On your silver anniversary here . . . Why tell that boy it's real silver when it cost all of $13?

(He goes over to RABBI SINGLETON.)

We have to talk, Rabbi. Our Board had a meeting . . . unanimous . . . sorry.

(He goes close to RABBI SINGLETON, fingers the rabbi's shirt.)

You got something on your shirt . . . any water around here?

RABBI SINGLETON

(Offering him the kiddush cup)

Just a little wine, not the solution of my problem. They met, you say?

BEN

(Bending over him at desk, sotto)

You'll . . . be okay . . . your daughter Terri wants you to retire, to enjoy life, to live with them in Florida, come down there. You deserve it after all these years in our shul . . .

(DANNY comes back. BEN pauses in front of him, looks back to RABBI SINGLETON, and leaves.)

RABBI SINGLETON

Ah, Danny. Galloping back so quick. Sit, please. Now take another look at this cup . . . ageless, like me.

RABBI SINGLETON (Cont'd)

(Pointing to a part of it)

Here, maybe, from ancient Egypt. You see the cracks in that corner? Very, very old. Now look. From Spain — still lasting from that cruel Inquisition, see? Over here some tears, and there, a little blood. See what that means?

(DANNY doesn't have a clue, nods politely. BEN reenters.)

See, when Moses and the rest left Spain . . .

BEN

So, how's the lesson going?

DANNY

(Straining)

Oh . . . exciting . . . guess I understand . . . a little.

BEN

(To himself)

We were afraid of that . . .

(Decisively)

Rabbi, may I speak with you . . . better, alone. You might want to go home, Daniel. It's getting dark . . .

RABBI SINGLETON

Now? I thought you . . .

BEN

Now.

(DANNY gets up eagerly.)

RABBI SINGLETON

But that will interrupt my sermon on the importance of free will — and choice. Do you mind waiting outside for a just a little—

BEN

Don't worry. He'll be back. You can finish with him . . .

DANNY

Well, in five minutes . . . I gotta help my grandma at home —

(He runs off. A pause.)

BEN

The Board thinks until June, to give you enough time to . . . Well . . . I mean . . . Rabbi, for years, you've done great service to this shul — Great.

RABBI SINGLETON

Yes, that's unquestionably correct.

BEN

The Board spoke so highly of you this evening . . . Rabbi . . . But by now . . . we think it may be all too much for you. You . . . uh, we have someone very qualified in mind to — carry on . . .

RABBI SINGLETON

Too much? For me?!? That is a misjudgment. A misinterpretation. Too much? In fact, it is too little! Life's too short!

BEN

But — Yes, well, at your advanced age —

RABBI SINGLETON

My age? No. How many milllenia . . . the Gentiles dream of Resurrection . . . Through me —
  (Lifts up the kiddush cup majestically)
Judaism shall sing of Rejuvenation!
  (Rises briskly from chair and does some brisk movement in place)
You looking? Hast thou beheld — No one — none—can replace me here!

BEN

Rabbi — Rabbi Singleton, please!

(After a second, RABBI SINGLETON stops. Silence.)

Rabbi —
  (Hesitantly)
Rabbi, do you remember just telling that young man—

RABBI SINGLETON

What?

BEN

No . . . well . . . forget it . . .

RABBI SINGLETON

No, what already?

RABBI SINGLETON (Cont'd)

(Silence)

WHAT—! You a spy of some sort like the boy says? Checking me out, like I'm some kind of grocery item?

BEN

Listen . . . Do you remember . . . saying to him . . . Moses left Spain—Moses —left from Spain?

RABBI SINGLETON

(Earnestly)

Well, yes, he did — well, figuratively.

(BEN puts his hand on RABBI SINGLETON's shoulder, recovering.)

Or the banks of the Nile . . . 0f course, they wouldn't lend Moses any money, so he went looking . . . for it . . . somewhere else . . . an old joke . . . old . . . His spirit left Spain —Why not? Good spirits always move on. Yes, no?

BEN

(Calls)

Danny . . . !

(To himself)

What am I going to do with you?

RABBI SINGLETON

Hmm. I used to say that about you, except even louder.

BEN

(To RABBI SINGLETON)

Don't! Please, don't make a total fool of yourself . . .

(DANNY reenters.)

Rabbi, you know how much the congregation likes you, but lately there've been complaints that you mix things up and —

RABBI SINGLETON

A Talmudic tradition — compare and contrast and —

BEN

But not confuse!

(Turning to DANNY)
Dannny . . . you told me when you were waiting to see the rabbi — that your folks got kind of mixed up when they were . . .

(He pauses to look at RABBI SINGLETON.)

DANNY
Actually, my grandma says she doesn't mind him, 'cause he's nice and deep, if we could understand him sometimes . . .

BEN
Uh, yes, we like him too and want to continue to like him, so Danny, we feel it would be an honor for you to be Rabbi Singleton's . . . last bar mitzvah student?

DANNY
Sure . . . I guess.

RABBI SINGLETON
(Recalling)
Yes . . . even the Pharaoh was ambushed . . . Now . . . Don, is it?

DANNY
Dan — my name's Dan —

RABBI SINGLETON
Right, Dan, I . . . don't always remember everything, but one thing I hope I never forget. See you next week, same time, uh, what is the time?

DANNY
4:30 —

RABBI SINGLETON
Alright. I'll write that down. Uh, where's a pencil?

(He finds one.)

Ah, good. We'll get into it, start going over your lines.

(DANNY nods, scampers out.)

RABBI SINGLETON
Did we decide what day?
(Shrugs)

RABBI SINGLETON (Cont'd)

God will tell us.

(Holding up the kiddush cup close to him, softly)

I dunno — maybe after all this — I know I'm 75, mazel tov. I could just hop down to Florida, hug my daughter and the kids — just sit and nosh and kibbitz with the trees.

(Sings)

Yeah, I talk to the trees.

(Speaks)

No more board meetings, no more checking up on me.

BEN

(Embarrassed)

Well, just for you, Rabbi, we could arrange a very generous . . . retirement package for you . . .

RABBI SINGLETON

Yeah, Ben, your packages always carry a lot of weight . . . but on the other hand — I don't know — you think maybe the kids don't understand me? I've heard you say that a lot . . . every day . . .

BEN

(Gently)

It's just not me. Remember what Danny's grandma said. People think you're —

RABBI SINGLETON

What? Not all there, or here? All the kids know that? With me, I thought they were, kinahora, not too bad . . . You did, remember when I taught you — how many years ago — even when I had to drag you in here sometimes . . . to study. Yes? I remember that. Do you? C'mon.

BEN

Yeah.

RABBI SINGLETON

Well, things worked out, you're the big man, now. So be big, meaning I don't know what, but, please, let's be clear — you're gonna have to drag my tuchus outta here — here, where I belong . . . at least for awhile, 'til I get to choose. Now you want to drink to that, Bennie?

(Blackout. MUSIC: Fade in reprise of light music opening)

The End

Late Bloomers

Allan Yashin

Photo by Andrew Benjamin

Dad can't believe his good fortune in dating Marilyn Monroe.

CHARACTERS:

Dad, 80s
Marilyn, his wife, same age
Paul, their son, early 60s
Amy, his wife, same age

TIME

An afternoon in spring

PLACE

Outside and inside he living room of a modest city apartment

(PAUL and AMY are by the outside door of his parents' apartment.)

PAUL

I know that they're my parents, but I want to make this visit quick.

AMY

I know. Quick like when we're making love.

PAUL

Please — let's not get into that again. Besides, I'm not the one who keeps the remote control in the bed.

AMY

I told you, the housekeeper must've put it under the pillow when she was straightening up.

PAUL

We wouldn't need a housekeeper if you weren't always at the gym with your friends.

AMY

Is your idea of a good exercise regimen for me staying home and doing the vacuuming and dusting for you?

PAUL

Then the least you could do is learn to cook. You haven't used the oven since you baked me a noodle pudding for my thirtieth birthday.

AMY

Oh, so while you're off on your millionth business trip of the year, I'm supposed to be home practicing my cooking.

PAUL

And if wasn't for my business trips, how would we afford your new BMW and your trips to that fancy spa in Colorado?

AMY

Well, at least I'm concerned about my appearance, which is more than I can say for . . .

PAUL

Shh! I can hear my father shuffling to the door. Remember, we just listen to why he wanted to speak to us and then you drive me to the airport. I gotta catch the 4:30 flight to Toledo.

AMY

Fine, but try to be more pleasant to your parents than you are to me. They're not getting any younger, you know.

PAUL

Yeah, I know. They're starting to worry me.

DAD

(Opening door)
My boy, Paulie and his beautiful wife Arlene!

PAUL

It's Amy, Dad. We've only been married for thirty-five years. You should know it by now.

DAD

A rose by any other name smells just as good — and so do you, Amy. Come give your father-in-law a big hug.

PAUL

Good to see you, Dad, good to see you . . . but I don't have much time, I've —

DAD

Ya' just got here. Relax! I got big news for you!

PAUL

Sure, sure, but let me say hello to Mom before you tell me.

DAD

Mom? Mom's gone.

AMY

What do you mean, Mom's gone?

DAD

Forget about Mom, will ya'? I don't know where she is.

AMY

Oh my goodness, I didn't realize he was that far gone.

PAUL

Come on, Dad, where did Mom go?

DAD

Would you stop talking and let me tell you why I asked you to come over today.

AMY

Okay, what is it, Dad?

DAD

I got a new girlfriend.

PAUL

Dad, what're you crazy? Mom's going to kill you!

DAD

I told you to forget about her! I have! And now I've got this new, hot dish and let me tell you . . . she's all over me!

PAUL

Who are you talking about?

AMY

Who is she?

DAD

It's Marilyn!

PAUL

Marilyn?

DAD

There's only one Marilyn! The beautiful, the voluptuous, the vivacious . . . Marilyn Monroe!

PAUL

It's worse than I thought!

AMY

He's lost it . . . he's really lost it!

DAD

I told her you were coming over to meet her today. Look — here she is now.

(An elderly woman in a blond wig wearing a housecoat comes out.)

MARILYN

(Hand on hip in a vixenish pose and speaking like"Marilyn")
Who is this lovely couple you've invited over?

AMY

Very cute, Mom. Now, why don't you take off the wig?

DAD

Wig? What wig?

PAUL

Stop that! It's not funny!

MARILYN

You want funny? You should watch me in *Some Like It Hot* — or *How To Marry A Millionaire*. I was quite a dish then.

DAD

Hubba, hubba!

PAUL

Would you two stop it! Marilyn Monroe's been dead for over twenty years!

MARILYN

That's what everybody thinks!

DAD

She faked it!

MARILYN

All those reporters, those photographers . . .

DAD

They hounded her, hounded her!

MARILYN

I just wanted to be left alone to read my Dostoyevsky. Arthur gave it to me after I divorced Joe D., and we've been happy as two lovebirds ever since.

AMY

Arthur? Who's Arthur?

DAD

Me! Arthur Miller! No seven-year itch for me — right, sweetiepie?

MARILYN

And Arthur and I got married by a rabbi, even though I'm not Jewish.

PAUL

Not Jewish! God help me!

MARILYN

Ooohhh, Artie! You're so strong and handsome — and such an intellectual, too!

PAUL

Amy, I can't handle this! Say something!

AMY

Look, Mom and Dad . . .

DAD and MARILYN

Who?

PAUL

You can't really be serious about all this?

MARILYN

Serious? They wouldn't let me be serious. They called me a dumb blonde. I'm not a dumb blonde, am I, Artie?

DAD

Of course not! You know I wrote *The Misfits* just for you. Now that was real dramatic acting. Why don't you go get your reviews?

MARILYN

Good idea! See what a smartie my Arthur is!

(MARILYN leaves the room.)

DAD

Paul . . . Amy . . . it's a sad, sad thing to see her this way.

PAUL

Oh, Dad . . . thank goodness . . . then at least you . . . you understand that she's . . .

DAD

Yes, that's she's not all there. I can still take care of her and I'll always love her, but just imagine . . .

PAUL

Imagine what, Dad?

DAD

That she thinks I'm Arthur Miller!

AMY

It must be very hard for you.

DAD

You know, the years go by so fast, you have to learn to cherish the time you have together while you can. But I'd better go check on her . . . can't leave her alone for too long.

(DAD leaves the room.)

AMY

I hate to bring this up, but if we don't leave soon, you'll miss your flight.

PAUL

My father's right. After seeing my parents like this, I realize I've been a fool . . . spending all that time away from home. We have to learn to take advantage of the time we have left together. Our marriage is very important to me.

AMY

Oh, Paul . . . and I promise to be a better wife to you instead of always thinking of ways to get away from the house.

(PAUL and AMY embrace.)

PAUL

Forget about the airport! Let's go home now . . . and I promise I'll be real slooow this time.

AMY

And I'll cook dinner afterwards . . . Better say goodbye to your parents.

PAUL

(Calling out to them)

Mom, Dad, we've gotta go now! But we'll see you again . . . real soon.

(PAUL and AMY leave.)

DAD

(Walking back into the living room with MARILYN)

They gave each other a big hug before they left.

MOM

(Taking off her wig and talking naturally)

That was a terrific idea you had.

DAD

It never would've worked without your great Marilyn Monroe impersonation.

MOM

It's good to see they can still learn a thing or two about life from us.

DAD

Maybe we're not too old to learn a thing or two from them.

MOM

Are you talking about what I hope you're talking about?

DAD

I can be real slooow too!

MOM

At our age, if it's too slow we'll both fall asleep in the middle.

DAD

Don't worry sweetheart, let's go to the bedroom. Artie will keep you awake.

MOM

Maybe just for tonight you could be Joe D. and bring your big Louisville Slugger with you.

DAD

As long as you bring your crucible!

(Blackout)

The End

Exit the Maven from Mott Haven

Milton Polsky

Photo by: Allan Yashin

Sheldon tries to convince his Uncle Morris to make a life-changing move.

CHARACTERS

Morris, a retired teacher, mid-70s
Sheldon, his nephew, a lawyer, about 40

TIME

Autumn, 2000, late afternoon. The sun is setting.

PLACE

A room in an apartment building located near Yankee Stadium, part of which can be seen in window to the right. The room is completely empty except for a little table with a phone on it.

(SHELDON, dressed casually in slacks and short-sleeved shirt, is putting the last things, including a stack of yellowed letters, in a suitcase while his UNCLE MORRIS stands at the window in deep repose.)

SHELDON
So this is all you're taking, Uncle Morris?

MORRIS
(Looking at the stack of letters SHELDON is about to put in suitcase)
What d'you want, a lifetime of heartaches and tsuris? Problems — got enough of . . .

SHELDON
Well, let's go, then.

MORRIS
Wait — more tsuris. I don't want to keep paying for the phone. You sure the — ?

SHELDON
(Assuring him)
Yeah, Margo took care of it —

MORRIS
You know, that is my one link to the world, you and Margo. You sure?

(SHELDON's cellphone rings. He takes it from his shirt pocket.)

SHELDON
Yeah, Margo — be right down.
(Looking at his watch)
Give us a couple of minutes . . . 'CAUSE IT'S HARD, THAT'S WHY! . . . Okay, sorry.

(The phone on the little table rings.)

MORRIS
They didn't turn it off! You said . . .

SHELDON
I know what I said.
(Into his cellphone)
You sure you got Uncle Morris's phone turned off? Okay. Then you talk to him . . .

(Picking up the other phone, which is still ringing.)
One minute, my wife will talk to you —

MORRIS

How can she . . . ?

SHELDON

(Putting his cellphone next to the phone on table)
Here, Margo, the phone company. Talk.

MORRIS

Oh . . .
(Pauses)
What they sayin' already?

(SHELDON shushes him assuredly as he continues to hold the cellphone into phone. During this, MORRIS drifts over to the window and then talks to SHELDON, who once in awhile listens in on the conversation.)

Look at it — Magnificent Yankee Stadium. That's why your Aunt — may she rest in peace — and I could see all those great games there. Man, there were some really great ones. Joe, Yogi, Billy . . . Whitey . . . *Something!* Incredible. Remember, I took you to a couple of games, remember that one time you were a kid, a little pisher — cryin' — your mother dropped you off here in Mott Haven, and I made you a promise *if you shut the f—up*, I'd get a ball for you — catch it, right — so I brought a glove, a mitt. I remember joking, it would be a mitzvah, you know, a good deed, if I caught it and you shut up. Well, I remember your sister brought along a glove, too, way too big for her little dainty fingers. Molly . . . Remember? And damn it if she didn't catch that gleaming white ball with the fine red stitchin'. How she doing, Molly? Huh, you still got it? I'm *talking*!

SHELDON

(Getting off the phone)
What?

MORRIS

Got it . . .

SHELDON

Yeah, they got it — You're off.

MORRIS

(Sadly)
Yeah . . .
(Pause)
You still got that ball?

SHELDON

What ball?

MORRIS

The one your sister caught. Your mother — my sister — she was so proud. Women's Lib — 1960s something, that year before Harold went off to Vietnam — Harold? What . . . Harold, why you do that . . . ?

SHELDON

Yeah . . . about Harold . . . sorry . . .

MORRIS

About the ball . . .

SHELDON

Cousin Harold . . .

MORRIS

(Sits in the chair.)
Killed your aunt, too — knew the minute she saw that envelope from the State Department that Harold was — broken heart, heartbreak and tsuris — that's what it's all about, right — ? The web of life. What did he say, my man, Shakespeare . . . ?

SHELDON

I guess. We got to go, Uncle Morris —

MORRIS

Got to? Who says? I can't leave so quick like a cow jumpin' over the moon, for godsakes. No, I don't want to leave.

(He gets up and drifts to window.)

I can still walk and breathe. C'mon, I'll take you and Marge to a game . . .

SHELDON

There's no game. Don't you know, the season is —
(Switches to a humoring tone)

Great — we'll go tomorrow. But first we have to —

MORRIS

(Perking up)
So we'll walk over there —

SHELDON

C'mon, Uncle Morris — I just told Margo —

MORRIS

You told her, so you think you can tell me — who are you to tell me anything, you? No, no. Look, everything changes, this building, the grounds, I used to have some friends around, and some of the kids I taught, but all I need to do is hop on the Number 4, and go anywhere I want.

SHELDON

We've been through it, Uncle Morris. You saw for yourself — it's a good place. They have good medical services, nice programs.

MORRIS

Me? Going where? Elizabeth, New Jersey, of all places? Yeah, a smelly dump. At least this place has character. Yeah. End it there. Can you figure that? "Glory is like a circle in the water, which never ceaseth to enlarge itself, till by broad spreading, it disperses . . . to naught." Henry. Six. Part One. Act One. Scene Two!

SHELDON

You know more about Shakespeare than anyone I know, Uncle Morris.

MORRIS

Maybe, and I taught it well, too . . . even to you, after Harold . . .

SHELDON

I know.

MORRIS

Did you know I named him after Harry — in Henry. Four — Hal — did you know that?

SHELDON

No.

MORRIS

He even talked about baseball, everything . . .

SHELDON

Harold . . .

MORRIS

Harold? No, *him*, Shakespeare. But it was tennis, tennis balls in Henry . . .
(Pauses)
Oh God, am I losing it? Tell me, talk to me, Harold! Why did you have to go to . . . The war was ending anyway, everyone was against it, but that bastard Nixon kept it going.
(Facing SHELDON)
Why? Harold? You know, right there, Harold, your mom couldn't stop crying when you told her you was going. Who understood it? Why? Because the kids are all going around here, you say. So what? You got a degree, I'm telling you — a degree, a degree! Why did you do it, Harold? Lotta people were getting out! You're a college graduate, for God's sake. People are saying to me, you teach school, How come he's going? Oh God, Harold.

SHELDON

(Holding MORRIS's hands)
I'm Sheldon.

(An uncomfortable pause. His cellphone rings and he talks into it.)

Yeah, yeah, yeah . . .

(He turns off his cellphone.)

MORRIS

Why doesn't she come up?

SHELDON

Double-parked. We gotta go.

(He takes suitcase and heads for the door.)

MORRIS

No wait, Harold . . . we never talk . . .

(SHELDON comes back to him.)

If anything happens, don't put it on me — I tried!

SHELDON

(Shaking him)
Uncle Morris!

MORRIS

So . . . how are things in your office? Sheldon? Sheldon.

SHELDON

Fine.

MORRIS

Doing well for yourself, huh? Lotta cases? Your degree paying off? Doing well?

SHELDON

(Modestly)
I guess. Enough to give me a headache. Big one.

(They laugh together.)

C'mon Uncle Morris, It's getting late . . .

(He puts his hand gently on MORRIS's shoulder, and MORRIS shucks it off quickly and forcefully.)

MORRIS

Wait a minute, we're not in one of your fancy courtrooms! This is a place — there are memories here, forty years of memories here, you think you can just toss that away like a ball or something. Your aunt and I had . . .
(As if in a daze)
. . . plenty of good times . . . your dad even used to come over, we played pinochle a little, talked about politics a lot . . . even from the lowest place — when virtuous things proceed — the place,the place, is dignified by the doer's deed —
(Long pause)
Can you put back the phone?

(SHELDON shakes his head "no.")

It got disconnected so fast, everything's happening so fast — everything.

(He moves to the telephone.)

The word "phony" . . .

SHELDON

What?

MORRIS

The word "phony" — because the first phones they made had a tinny effect — phony. No, not Edison — Bell — like the cookie, Graham something . . . Good man. Worked with deaf people, he did. Edison had tsuris with his ears, y'know?

SHELDON

Uncle Morris, you're a real maven, the maven of Mott Haven. You know it all.

MORRIS

Yeah? So a lotta good that'll do me where I'm going — where you're taking me!

SHELDON

(Trying to be reassuring)

No, don't say that. Don't worry, you'll like it.

MORRIS

How do you know? You a maven too?

(Another pause).

I said, how do you know? Talk! You hard of hearing, too?

SHELDON

Uh, well — you'll see — they have a Shakespeare class there.

MORRIS

What?

SHELDON

They have a . . .

MORRIS

I heard you, I heard you. Shakespeare, for real? Why didn't you tell me, you, zhlub. Lawyers, you never get around to the real thing.

(Excited)

Hmm . . . For this I got to go to the bathroom! You wait right there.

(He goes off. Cellphone rings again.)

SHELDON

(Into cellphone, in exasperated whisper)

SHUT THE FUCK UP! We're coming down!

(Controlling himself)

He keeps on talking about my cousin Harold.

(Pause)

Look, in the car, back me up — tell him they have a Shakespeare Club at the retirement home. . . . How do I know? I had to say something. . . . I swear I'll teach the fucking course myself, if that's the only way, I'll do it! . . . Okay, okay, right down!

(SHELDON turns off cellphone as MORRIS re-enters the room. He is wearing a Yankee baseball cap.)

MORRIS

Let's go. Hark, hear that flushing? A most Royal Flush, as Shakespeare did say well . . . thither —

(Moodily)

To be dispatched . . .

SHELDON

Look . . .

MORRIS

What?

SHELDON

I'm trying!

MORRIS

Yeah?

SHELDON

Yeah!

(Calming down)

C'mon, we have to go. Now.

MORRIS

I know we do, Harold. Well, don't worry. I don't have to teach after school today. C'mon, c'mon. We'll be late to the game. Look what I got you — it's a brand new ball. You like It? C'mon, we'll be late for the game, Harold.

SHELDON

Then we'd better hurry, Dad — the game'll be starting any minute.

MORRIS

One minute, one minute — not so fast, son — you be Bob Feller, I'll be Joltin' Joe —

(SHELDON winds up to pitch, delivers, MORRIS misses.)

SHELDON

That's strike one!

MORRIS

Crmon, Bob! Try to get me out — come on — can't do it, can you?

SHELDON

Who says I can't?

(He winds up to pitch again.)

MORRIS

C'mon, a hundred miles an hour! C'mon —

(SHELDON winds up with gusto. MORRIS hits it.)

SHELDON

Pop-up . . . foul!

MORRIS

(Softly but determinedly)
Don't worry, I'm hanging . . .

(SHELDON winds up again, trying harder. MORRIS swings the bat with gusto.)

SHELDON

It's a high fly — it's going, going . . . it is *gone* — into the left field stands for a home run!

(They both laugh, as they follow the flight of the ball. Then SHELDON abruptly stops. MORRIS stops. A pause. SHELDON and MORRIS face at each other for a few seconds. Then SHELDON picks up the suitcase, slowly, at first, then with more resolve.)

C'mon, Dad.

(MORRIS turns and follows SHELDON as they make their way to the door.)

MORRIS

Coming, Harold . . .

(SHELDON takes MORRIS's hand, but MORRIS gently brushes it away, as so exits the maven from Mott Haven.)

(Fade out)

The End

The Pre-Bre Agreement

Allan Yashin

Photo by Andrew Benjamin

A tough negotiation is underway.

CHARACTERS

Sam, 60s
Sara, his wife, 60s

TIME

Today

PLACE

Their expensively furnished dining room

(SAM and SARA are sitting side by side at the dining room table.)

SAM

Now I'm going to draw a line down the middle of this legal pad and on one side I'll write MINE.

(He writes 'MINE' on the legal pad.)

And on the other side I'll write YOURS . . .

(He does this also.)

SARA

Wait a minute! That makes it seem as though you have some proprietary stake here.

SAM

Proprietary stake! What's with the ten-dollar words all of a sudden?

SARA

Oh, and you're the only one with a college degree in this family?

SAM

If you want to count Brooklyn College, then go ahead.

SARA

Well, with you using the MINE column for yourself, it looks like you're making all the decisions.

SAM

Look, if we can't even get past deciding how to label the columns, we'll never accomplish anything.

SARA

Well, I'm only trying to look after my interests.

SAM

So, you think I don't have your interests at heart?

SARA

So, if you have my interests at heart, why are we making a Pre-Nup agreement after thirty years of marriage?

SAM

Please, Sara, it's not a Pre-Nup, it's a Pre-Bre, a Pre-Breakup Agreement. Our attorney suggested it, and I think it could potentially save us a lot of bitter feelings.

SARA

Pre-Breakup, I don't like the whole idea. It sounds so fatalistic and defeatist.

SAM

Darling, you know I could never imagine living without you . . . but just in case.

SARA

Just in case of what?

SAM

Well, in case you meet a younger man, let's say, and decide you want to move out. In addition to my broken heart, I don't want to have to start fighting over the dividing of our assets. We should do that now. So, let's start. Yours and mine, all right? So, I'll take the house and put it under MINE.

SARA

Wait a minute! The house! Why should you get the house?

SAM

Well, if you're going to run off with a younger man . . .

SARA

But, that's just a hypothetical situation you made up!

SAM

Well, I've seen you staring at the message therapist at the gym.

SARA

That's crazy! Just because his tuches looks good in sweatpants doesn't mean I'm planning to run away with him.

SAM

Oh . . . so you've noticed his ass!

SARA

At least I don't make a fool of myself over him like you do with that little shiksa barista down at Starbucks. She's got to hose down the counter after you're finished drooling over her while she's making your latte. Give me the damn house on my side of the legal pad!

SAM

All right, Sara, all right! But I'm going to have to take something of equal value.

SARA

Go ahead, but don't be greedy.

SAM

Oh, that hurts, really hurts! After all these years you actually think I'd take more than's coming to me. Look, all I'm taking for myself is the stock portfolio.

SARA

Like hell you are! My parents gave us that portfolio.

SAM

Yes, and your brother, the so-called investment maven, lost over half of it already. I'm taking the rest while there's still some left.

SARA

Do I insult your family that way? Do I bring up your father's drinking . . . or your mother's face job that looks like her cheekbones are made out of Play Dough . . . or your sister appearing on "Wet and Wild Housewives of Massapequa"? Do I? No, I do not! I'm taking the Mercedes . . . both of them.

SAM

If that's the way you want to be . . . then I'm taking the grandchildren!

SARA

You're taking the grandchildren? We don't have any grandchildren.

SAM

Well, it's only a matter of time. Did you see that little bulge on our daughter's stomach last week? And the way she and that son-in law of ours of kept smiling at each other? I think they're going to have an announcement to make shortly.

SARA

(Softening)

Do you really think so?

(Taking SAM's hand)
Oh, that would be wonderful! Do you think it'll be a boy or a girl?

SAM

Boys run in the family, dear, so you can start knitting blue booties soon.

SARA

Oh, I can hardly wait!

SAM

Good. You can take the booties. I'm taking the grandchildren!

SARA

Don't be ridiculous! They're people, not inanimate objects. You can't own them!

SAM

I'm talking about seeing them on the holidays. I'm taking them for Hanukkah!

SARA

Okay, Mr. Wiseguy! There are eight days of Hanukkah, so I'm taking them for Thanksgiving, New Year's Day, and Passover.

SAM

Are you crazy? That's all the rest of the good days. What're you leaving me?

SARA

You can have them on Yom Kippur.

SAM

Is that supposed to be a joke? I'm in temple most of the day, and besides, after not eating and drinking all day, my breath smells.

SARA

You're telling me!

SAM

Well, maybe if you'd stop cooking those salmon croquettes with garlic sauce the night before, I wouldn't smell so much. What kind of a dinner is that to make when I can't drink for twenty-four hours?

SARA

That happens to be my bubbe's own recipe, and I consider myself an excellent cook, if you don't mind! As a matter of fact, put all my cookbooks and recipes on my side of the list. I'm taking them!

SAM

You can't have them.

SARA

And why is that?

SAM

The CIA took them. They're going to use them to replace waterboarding.

SARA

If you think you're such a comedian, maybe you'll get a laugh out of the fact that I'm taking the housekeeper.

SAM

Well, since you're so messy and disorganized you probably should keep her.

SARA

I'm keeping her because you won't need a housekeeper since I'm getting the house, not you.

SAM

Oh, so you're assuming I'll be living in a one-room subterranean hovel with imitation wood paneling and one street-level window.

SARA

That's probably all you'll be able to afford after the alimony you'll be paying me.

SAM

Alimony! You're expecting me to pay you alimony? After all these years screaming about equality for women, you want me to support you?

SARA

And aren't you the one who kept me from having a career all these years?

SAM

Okay, then here's a chance for you to finally take advantage of that degree you got from Brooklyn College.

SARA

So you want me to support myself? Then you know a bachelor's degree is worthless nowadays. Put an MBA from Columbia in my column — and you're paying for it!

SAM

Send you to Columbia . . . Sure, of course, why not? But then I won't be able to continue paying those outrageous life insurance premiums that would've left you the second richest woman in America when I died.

SARA

Still complaining about those insurance premiums, after all these years. I suppose you really don't care what happens to me when you're gone.

SAM

You can always move into my subterranean hovel.

SARA

That's not funny!
(Starting to get teary-eyed)
You're being mean to me!

SAM

(Suddenly contrite)
Now there, dear. No need to be upset. You know, maybe this Pre-Bre Agreement isn't such a good idea. I guess I'm just no King Solomon. Look, I'm going to throw it away.

(SAM tears up the Agreement)

After all . . . we get along so well there's no reason to think we'd *ever break up.*

(Blackout)

The End

Production History of the Plays

Rhineland Bastard was presented in November, 2010, as a staged reading by the UFT Players in New York City, directed by Elizabeth Rosen. It was published in *Jewish Currents* in March, 2013.

First We Have The Bris, Then We Eat The Brisket was performed in June, 2013, in New York City as part of the "It's a Laugh: Original Plays of Allan Yashin Festival," presented by the East Side Players in New York City. The staged reading was directed by Lolly Yacker Winderbaum.

Shakes Hands was presented as a staged reading by the UFT Players in New York City on April 24, 2009, directed by Suzanne Lamberg. The play was published in *A Shakespeare Trilogy*, Puck Press, Inc. in 2011.

A Chance Encounter was performed as a staged reading by the East Side Players on June 28, 2014, and was directed by the author.

I Feel Their Pain was presented as a staged reading by *Around the Block* in April, 2012. In June, 2013, in New York City. It was performed as part of the "It's a Laugh: Original Plays of Allan Yashin Festival," presented by the East Side Players. In November, 2013, it was given four performances in a fully staged production directed by Andreas Robertz for the ATB Play Festival, New York City.

A Stroll In the Garden was rewritten as one of the scenes in *Sail On, Seniors!* presented as a staged reading by the UFT Players, New York City, in November, 2013, and directed by Lolly Yacker Winderbaum. It was performed in June, 2014, by the East Side Players, directed by the author.

Mister Mitzvah Maker, directed by the author, was presented on February 22, 2013, by the East Side Players in February, 2014.

The Empty Seder Chair, was presented as a staged reading by the East Side Players in New York City in February, 2014, directed by the author.

Chekhov-Shmekhov was performed in June, 2013, as part of the "It's a Laugh: Original Plays of Allan Yashin Festival," presented by the East Side Players. The play was directed by the author.

The Polish Girl was presented as a staged reading by the East Side Players on June 28, 2014, directed by the author.

The Kiddush Cup was performed as a staged reading by the East Side Players on June 28, 2014, directed by the author.

The Late Bloomers was presented as a staged reading at "The Raymond Flores Short Play Festival" on June 7, 2014, and at the "Queens UFT End-Year Festival" in June, 2013.

Exit the Maven from Mott Haven was first produced as a staged reading by The UFT Players in New York City in the late 1990s. It was directed by the author. It was also produced in a Manhattan library in the early 2000s. It was a winner of a national playwriting contest sponsored by Patv (Public Access Tv Corp), directed by Norman Hall. The play was subsequently broadcast on cable television and was also selected as a winner in an original play national television competition.

The Pre-Bre Agreement was presented as a staged reading by the UFT Players, New York City, in June, 2011, directed by the author.

More Plays by the Authors

These produced plays on related themes of the book are available in manuscript format. Please email Milton at polskyspen@aol.com or Allan at AY100641@aol.com to inquire how to obtain copies.

Losing Control
In Allan's full-length comedy, after a lifetime of fighting for social equality, will Irv sell out his principles to help ensure the financial future of his dear nephew on the newly gentrified Lower East Side?

Shoeless in Union Square
In Milt's one-act comedy-drama, on the eve of December 1, 1955, before a celebration of Rosa Parks in New York's Union Square Park, two former Russian revolutionary comrades meet unexpectedly after a 50-year separation and recall partaking in the 1905 radical demonstrations in Saint Petersburg Square in Russia — and compare their lives in America since then.

Loved Him Like a Father
Allan's full-length comedy about strained family relationships when step-brothers disagree about whether or not to sell the home of their deceased parents in Florida.

The Reunion
Milt's one-actor is about a single, lonely composer who, on the night of sitting *shiva* for his mother, is reunited with a former non-Jewish woman whom he hasn't seen in 30 years—after his mother stopped their high school romance that was heating up.

The Seder
Published by Players Press, Inc., POB 1132, Studio City, CA 91514 (playerspress@attn.net)
In Milt's two-act play, a union organizer climbs his way up to become a powerful clothing manufacturer in a period covering 50 years full of promise, heartache, and hope. Each personal scene covers a life-changing event in local, national, or world history.

The Water Cure
In Milt's one-act drama, in Toledo, Spain in 1584, Father Alexis, assigned to the Spanish Inquisition there, attempts to force his resistant brother, a young Jesuit priest, to accept all the tenets of the Inquisition, even as a teenage *converso* is being tortured in the next room.

Robin Hoodwinked

Allan's comedy follows George's attempt to pass himself off as a Latino in order to take advantage of "minority hiring" to get a new job, until a letter from the "Prince of Nigeria" changes his plans.

About the Authors

Photo by Roberta Polsky

Dr. Milton Polsky is a prize-winning playwright and author of *You Can Write a Play* and *A Shakespeare Trilogy*. He has taught playwriting at the City University of New York and New York University, where he was a Shubert Fellow in Playwriting. He serves as co-chair of the UFT Players, where a number of his plays and musicals have been produced. He is also the co-author, with Warren Wyss, of the mystery novel *Shadows on Bleecker Street.*

Allan Yashin has had more than a dozen of his plays produced in various performing arts spaces in the New York City area. His plays have been staged by the Obie Award-sharing ABT, as well as by the East Side Players. A number of his plays have been performed by the UFT Players, of which he is a member of the executive board. He is also the author of the suspense novel *Protected.*